Through Blurred Vision

THROUGH BLURRED VISION

Claiming Victory
in All Aspects of Life

KURT
PANGBORN

NASHVILLE

NEW YORK • LONDON • MELBOURNE • VANCOUVER

Through Blurred Vision
Claiming Victory in All Aspects of Life

© 2022 Kurt Pangborn

Published in New York, New York, by Morgan James Publishing. Morgan James is a trademark of Morgan James, LLC. www.MorganJamesPublishing.com

Proudly distributed by Ingram Publisher Services

Morgan James BOGO™

A **FREE** ebook edition is available for you or a friend with the purchase of this print book.

CLEARLY SIGN YOUR NAME ABOVE

Instructions to claim your free ebook edition:
1. Visit MorganJamesBOGO.com
2. Sign your name CLEARLY in the space above
3. Complete the form and submit a photo of this entire page
4. You or your friend can download the ebook to your preferred device

ISBN 9781631958175 paperback
ISBN 9781631958182 ebook
Library of Congress Control Number:
2021949475

Cover & Interior Design by:
Christopher Kirk
www.GFSstudio.com

Morgan James PUBLISHING Builds with... Habitat for Humanity Peninsula and Greater Williamsburg

Morgan James is a proud partner of Habitat for Humanity Peninsula and Greater Williamsburg. Partners in building since 2006.

Get involved today! Visit MorganJamesPublishing.com/giving-back

I dedicate Through Blurred Vision *to my Lord and Savior Jesus Christ. I'm simply living out his design for my life and want to bring honor and glory to his name. It is my burden and hope that this book will point individuals to Christ and touch a world encompassed in darkness. True love, wisdom, and peace in this life come from a personal relationship with God. All I am and all I have is directly connected to Christ. I commit* Through Blurred Vision *to the Lord to further the kingdom and encourage fellow believers in their faith.*

TABLE OF CONTENTS

ACKNOWLEDGMENTS

I t brings me immense joy to acknowledge the following individuals who have been instrumental in my life. Their impact is all-encompassing and touches every part of who I am. Each of their investments has contributed to the creation of *Through Blurred Vision.*

Rosie Dellinger—It is widely known that "there is no love on earth as powerful as a mother's love" is illuminated to its fullest extent in my life. My mother carried me, fought for me, uplifted me, and molded me through her teaching. All the while she faced the adversity of turning from parental religious convictions, loneliness, and the unknown world of congenital glaucoma. Her firm leadership, yet genuine being, eclipsed each breaking point that could have led to failure. This season of writing has only enhanced my love and admiration for my mother. My aim is to reflect the same love and direction in my own life, as I know this aim is intended for the highest level.

Dr. Forrest D. Ellis—Now a member of the Pediatric Ophthalmology and Strabismus Hall of Fame, Dr. Ellis conducted more than thirty operations on my eyes. He was—and is—truly a pioneer in the field of congenital glaucoma. A striking professionalism was not only demonstrated in the operating room but he was also a genuine spirit in the examination room. My file was carried across the country, to multiple physicians, and even into his home all for the cause of salvaging a portion of my sight. His tireless nights and efforts enabled me to keep the gift of sight. My upmost appreciation and respect to Dr. Forrest D. Ellis.

Clif Marshall—God uses His people for His glory! I met Clif in the west lobby of Simon Skjodt Assembly Hall shortly after he was hired as Director of Performance for Men's Basketball at Indiana University. Clif was taking independent time to learn his new surroundings, and I was happy to assist him. In February of 2018, I sent him a text asking if we could meet. I knew the Holy Spirit was directing me to talk with him about starting a bible study and/or prayer group in athletics. Predicting this leading was meant for others, but it was also meant for me. Through Christ's love, Clif pressed me to share my complete testimony. *Through Blurred Vision* is the entire revelation of my testimony, because Clif (being used by God) said it was time to share. Clif is not only a close friend but the mentor God knew I needed.

Morgan James Publishing—I would like to thank the entire Morgan James team for an incredibly smooth process.

They have demonstrated complete support and encouragement through this process. As a new author, they made me feel at home and shared in the excitement for my testimony and message. I am blessed to have such a great publisher who cares about pushing the gospel forward. I look forward to many years of service together!

Aubrey Kosa—I am extremely grateful for Aubrey's commitment and investment as it pertains to professionally editing my manuscript. Aubrey's ability to see my heart and deliver my testimony in the clearest manner is sincerely appreciated. Aubrey has played a crucial role in bringing *Through Blurred Vision* to a complete form.

Chad Pangborn—A perfect representation of God's design, care, and purpose is found in my brother, Chad. Like myself, Chad was also diagnosed with congenital glaucoma at a young age. His condition was not as advanced, thus requiring less medical intervention. Yet, Chad has been there every step of the way and shares the journey with me. From comparing our eye pressures with NASCAR driver numbers to the operating table and into the courtroom, he stands as my best friend. Today and every day I continually stand in amazement for Chad's quiet, yet strong, presence that pulled me through the deepest of sorrows. Navigating new waters throughout my childhood, Chad not only swam beside me but also kept my head above the swirling waters.

Dr. Hemang C. Patel—Unto this day, Dr. Patel continues to provide tremendous support and council as my glaucoma specialist. Through regular examinations and determinations, I've been able to maintain limited vision in both eyes.

His work has allowed me to continue to pursue my career aspirations and enjoy the benefits of sight. I cannot thank him enough for his continued work and friendship that makes the medical process behind glaucoma smooth and gives me peace of mind.

FOREWORD

If you only look at us, you might well miss the brightness. We carry this precious Message around in the unadorned clay pots of our ordinary lives. That's to prevent anyone from confusing God's incomparable power with us. As it is, there's not much chance of that. You know for yourselves that we're not much to look at. We've been surrounded and battered by troubles, but we're not demoralized; we're not sure what to do, but we know that God knows what to do; we've been spiritually terrorized, but God hasn't left our side; we've been thrown down, but we haven't broken. What they did to Jesus, they do to us—trial and torture, mockery and murder; what Jesus did among them, he does in us—he lives! Our lives are at constant risk for Jesus' sake, which makes Jesus' life all the more evident in us. While we're going through the worst, you're getting in on the best!
–2 Corinthians 4:8–11 (MSG)

xiv | **THROUGH BLURRED VISION**

A fter a couple of casual meetings that took place while Kurt was giving a tour of Indiana University, it became obvious to me that we were a couple of Hoosiers who have much more in common than just growing up in the same hometown. We both have a "precious Message" that we carry around in our "unadorned clay pots," and we are ready and willing to share it with anyone who will listen.

Kurt's courageous battle with blindness has given him a story that parallels how some are blinded by Satan from believing the gospel message about Jesus. Kurt's life displays his commitment to God and his belief in God's promises, even when the journey is hard. His story provides a guide for living a life that is grounded in praise, prayer, and perseverance. This account is a testimony of how Kurt Pangborn's faith and trust in God's plan consistently sustained him through forty eye surgeries and other tough obstacles throughout his life.

This book provides hope that God's sovereignty is always at work in our lives even when we struggle to wrap our human minds around the path God is leading us through, especially when our plan does not look like His plan for our lives.

Through Blurred Vision is a vulnerable attempt to share a bold message, and I am thankful Kurt had the courage and the discipline to write it. The good news contained in this book has the power to open blind eyes to the truth of who Jesus is and to encourage believers who have lost sight of their purpose in life.

Tom Allen
Husband, father, and head football coach at Indiana University

AUTHOR'S NOTE

First and foremost, *Through Blurred Vision* is my testimony—my open acknowledgment and firsthand account of my walk with Christ. As an infant, I was given the unexpected diagnosis of congenital glaucoma, a diagnosis that followed me as I grew up and into adulthood. Here in these pages, I share my life and a story that expounds upon the physical, emotional, and relational struggles that came with my diagnosis.

But this is not a story that ends in brokenness.

Through a life-changing moment of conviction, a new life was revealed for a mother faced with unsurmountable challenges and a son with an unknown future, and now I am compelled to share that conviction—and the Word of God that sparked it—with the world.

In this book, I encourage you to claim victory and step into higher living. You are part of a grand design. You have a much greater purpose than yourself, but blurred vision—a condition I believe entangles every man, woman, son, and daughter—prevents most people from discovering that purpose.

While this is my story, I also provide practical tools to sharpen your faith toward the end of the book, along with my three Ps to help you set a game plan for each day. I pray that through Christ's love, my testimony illuminates your light, life, and grander purpose.

Chapter 1

GREATER THAN THE LIMITATION

For with God nothing shall be impossible.
—Luke 1:37

Withholding, restrictive, impeded from advancing as one could or desperately desires—all expressive words that are connected to the root word "limitation." Each one of us has encountered a limitation in our life's journey, but you would be hard-pressed to find someone who would voluntarily add a limitation to their life. Accepting the limitations or not, we reside in a world populated with individuals who have a story marked by limitation. Produced by birth, betrayal, brokenness, or a combination of the three, limitations seem to easily press on our journey.

Subtle reminders often linger that limitations do, in fact, exist. Envision yourself driving down the highway. Along the edge of the road, you notice signs that indicate the appropriate speed limit. By law you are required to maintain the posted speed; failure to comply can result in a violation, fine, or devastating outcome. Your car's dashboard may have a max reading of 140 miles per hour, but the road sign indicates you must stay at sixty-five miles per hour. You may eagerly want to cut down on travel time, but the speed limitation cannot be overlooked.

On the issue of time, do you ever find yourself needing more hours in the day? No matter where you live or who you are, a day only has 1,440 minutes, or twenty-four hours. Pressed by a deadline or overwhelmed with a laundry list of tasks, time quickly escapes. "If I only had more time" is a limitation that chimes true on every watch.

Or consider the lack of sweetness with a limitation. If you make the decision to treat yourself to a hot fudge sundae, of course you want to add the crushed pecans and whipped cream and top it off with a cherry. But while waiting to place your order, you see a sign that reads: "One free small cone." Being the fiscally responsible person you are, your mind starts to shift away from the sundae until you read the fine print: "Child's height must be under forty inches." Now, to the amusement of fellow customers, you could crouch down trying to meet the height requirements. Yet, knowing yourself, it would be likely that you would simply fall over trying to obtain a free ice cream cone. Chuckling at the thought, you move forward with ordering the hot fudge sundae, realizing sweetness cannot be found in the posted limitation.

But could it be possible that the limitations in our lives end up enhancing them? Can your darkest night precede your brightest day? Would it be acceptable for a heart to be full of joy facing the gift of a limitation?

Most people would meet those questions with raised eyebrows and a certain level of opposition. After all, limitations are classified by words such as restrictive, withholding, and impeding; they highlight the downfall or weakness in an individual's life. Cast to the side by society, limitations are labeled hindrances. Many collapse under the weight of a limitation and struggle to find a way forward, crushed by just the emotion of the limitation. The pain is real, and the discontent lies heavy as a lead blanket for millions of individuals today—including me. I was once distraught by the path I found myself on. Why was I placed in the 0.0001 percent of the population who had to face this lifelong trial? Without real, scientific answers, it seemed I had been given an extremely unfair set of circumstances.

We must understand that the "speed limits" of life are placed by God for our protection; his timing is always perfect, no matter how we perceive it. And yes, sweetness can be connected to those limitations. You see, God's subtraction is actually a form of addition. He wants to use an adverse situation to show that He is strong. What we perceive as unfair or a position with no options can lead us to a God who has no limitations. Psalms 121:4 tells us that God shall neither slumber nor sleep. He is fully aware of each and every person's situation and will never close His eyes on your life. Nothing is impossible with God!

Rejoice that limitations—past, present, and future—do not hinder what God can and will do in your life! When you place absolute faith in His word, the limitation quickly becomes second to the lesson, and that lesson is transformed into a message. God's grace is a spectacular work in and through our lives, which changes the sight of a limitation into a vision for His goodness.

Admittedly, this viewpoint did not align with my heart or conviction for many years. In my case, the limitations simply seemed far too great. There were many years when I would have called you a liar if I had read the above paragraph. I couldn't wrap my mind around the possibility that my limitation was a gift and could lead to an opportunity. Being self-absorbed, I was willing to lock my life in a room and participate in a sorrow tour that would have circled me around to the same position each and every year.

As you read and intercede with your own thoughts, adjust your perspective on your own journey. Claim the hurt, disappointments, and all the shortcomings, for you no longer must be weary. As daunting as the climb may seem, sacrificing a life of victory to independently patch life together isn't worth it. Let us build a bridge to the promise of victory! *Through Blurred Vision*, you will rise in celebration and refocus on a new foundation for your purpose.

Chapter 2

UNEXPECTED ANTICIPATION
TO DEVASTATION

Tucked away in east central Indiana was a farming community where my mother was born and raised. (To be clear, the closest town was named Farmland.) My mother was raised alongside three sisters and two brothers. Their living arrangements were those you associate with a long time ago or with Amish customs. Devout in their Christian faith, my mother's community chose seclusion over society. The family was very frugal and lived simply. I remember my mom offering stories about sharing bathwater, working in the garden, wearing pantyhose that you could see dust fly from, and finding entertainment in the outdoors. My grandmother eventually started a church, which would also serve as the local school. Opposing the public schools' teachings, they wanted an education that would focus on the basics combined with biblical principles. From the back bedroom window of their home, you could easily see the schoolhouse/church.

You must understand that traveling outside of their community was a rarity. My mom and her siblings lived a sheltered life, one that experienced truly little influence from the outside world. Dinning in a restaurant, visiting the doctor for an appointment, or meeting friends in the community almost never happened. Medical intervention was completely frowned upon, and it was something they decided to go without due to religious convictions. Everything they understood about the world and were taught came from within the small circle of home and school.

Advancing into her teenage years, my mom began to take on responsibilities not only at home, but outside of home as well. She accepted a babysitting job for a neighbor who lived around the corner. This family owned a dairy farm (where she would later meet my dad). At that time, my dad was employed by his father, who owned a milk transport business. They ran routes daily to pick up milk from local dairy farms and transport it to the processing plant.

During a scheduled stop at the farm where my mom was babysitting, my parents happened to cross paths. Conversations progressed, and a certain level of interest arose. Considering that it would seem highly inappropriate to my mom's parents for their daughter to be involved in dating, they labeled the process as courting. They believed you only talk to the opposite sex with pure intentions of marriage. Talking to a man meant that you were interested in having a long-term future; otherwise, you were simply leading him on. As the days passed, my mom and dad started to spend time together outside of his visits to the farm.

(Of course, keep in mind this was all brand-new for my mother. She had very little experience going to town, dining out, and having public entertainment options.)

As days turned into weeks, my grandmother began to pressure my mom, asking if she had true feelings for my dad. Truthfully, my mom's focus was not on finding a life partner but rather enjoying freedom for the very first time. Mom was simply having fun and loving the ability to leave her restrictive life. I chuckle when I imagine my mom waiting to change into blue jeans until she had left the house since appropriate attire for a woman meant a long dress with no jewelry or accessories. Bringing attention to yourself was seen as prideful—a worldly mindset. With enjoyment on one side and restrictive pressure on the other, it is easy to see why my mom gravitated toward my dad. It wasn't love or attraction; it was a new lease on life.

I imagine my dad saw an opportunity while my mom became increasingly angry about her indoctrination at home, and in a moment of opportune circumstance, my mom made the quick decision to leave home and move in with my dad. She was met with extreme opposition from her parents. In fact, they told her that she would no longer be part of the family. But disconnected or not, my mom went forward with leaving home for the very first time.

After she moved in with my dad, she started assisting him on his milk routes. Later he asked for her hand in marriage, but my mom was not happy even on her wedding day. She felt like there was no one to turn to and no place for her to go after her upbringing and experiencing her family turning their backs on her. She didn't know how to annul a marriage or seek help. Mom knew it was a big mistake to take her vows, but she resided alone on an island. Absorbed in the idea that she had made her bed and must lie in it, there was no turning around. From the onset, every situation in my parents' marriage seemed undervalued. My dad did not want to move out of his parents' house, he didn't want to go on a honeymoon, and he was more concerned about running the milk route than spending time with his new wife.

Their journey did not get any simpler when my mom experienced an ectopic pregnancy. My mom was rushed through emergency surgery as the case proved to be life-threatening, and physicians advised her that it was highly unlikely she would be able to bear children following the procedure. She struggled to come to grips with the inability to have her own kids. How extremely painful it is for a woman to be told she cannot bring forth new life. I can imagine my mom's struggle in the pain and the discontent that laid heavy upon her heart. I believe she probably deemed this to be a curse for her disobedience to her parents' wishes. But the doctor's statement would be nullified when my mom found out that she was pregnant. Filled with joy and excitement, my mom began to think about what it would be like to be a mom. Once faced with never having her own children, she was now looking at a future connected to her own child. On an extremely hot August 3, she gave birth to an 8-pound, 8.5-ounce baby boy.

Abounding in joy, my mom held her very own baby boy right there in the Henry County Memorial Hospital. And in those precious moments, her attention was drawn to the eyes and their grayish blue tint. They did not seem to be clear or appear normal as a mother would expect. While a mother's instinct placed a question in her mind, she tried not to wrestle with the thought as she continued to enjoy time with her brand-new baby boy.

As daylight broke on August 4, so would a new direction for a mother and her son. The doctor's shoes clipped along the floor as he entered the room to check in. Stating that all seemed to be well with my mom's health, the doctor began to provide an update on her baby: "You have a very healthy boy, but ..."

Captivated and concerned by the word "but," my mom held her breath, not really wanting to hear the next few words. She had a suspicion the night before when she looked into my eyes, and the doctor confirmed it by recommending a specialist in Indianapolis. Paperwork was sent to the rotary building, which connected to Riley Children's Hospital. It was there my mom would later meet Dr. Forrest Ellis for an examination and detailed review of any eye condition present. August 8 was the date of the initial interaction between Dr. Ellis and my mother, and my eye pressures were listed at 48 and 52 (normally the eye pressures should at least be below 20, if not in the mid-teens). The diagnosis was provided; I had congenital glaucoma. Mom, being completely caught off guard, spoke up, "I thought glaucoma is only in older adults?"

Dr. Ellis replied, "Well, in fact, it is, but it can also appear in infants." Without slowing down, Dr. Ellis continued to explain that immediate intervention was necessary. My eye pressures could not remain that high, and it would require an emergency operation. Before my mom could process the information, we were whisked through the underground tunnel that would lead to Riley Children's Hospital. Here was a mom who grew up in rural Indiana with a strict background now faced with a dire situation surrounding her blessing of a baby boy. Prepping for surgery, so many questions were racing through my mom's mind, but at that very moment, she had to put her full trust in the doctor's wisdom. Praise God that my mom decided to fight for my vision and accept medical intervention at such a crucial crossroads.

Reasons do not exist for why I was diagnosed with congenital glaucoma. It was impossible to trace or link glaucoma on either side of my family with no record of glaucoma as far as either side of the family could remember.

The best way to describe the emotions that my mom encountered is exactly like a roller coaster. She went from expecting no children of her own to becoming pregnant and delivering her first child only for him to receive a terrible diagnosis. Devastation had struck twice—how long was this devastation going to linger? Would the operation be successful in lowering the pressures? How much could her son see? How much had his eyes been damaged? A nightmare took on the look of Riley Children's Hospital. As the doctors fervently worked in the operating room, a mom sat squeezing her hands in fear.

Chapter 3

SUDDEN BLUR

Receiving the diagnosis of congenital glaucoma meant I was in the 0.0001 percent of the population that received that diagnosis. For a new mother, this was the ultimate feeling of being trapped in the desert all alone. Where could you turn to find answers? More importantly, what were the chances that her son would be able to see? Had too much damage been done prior to birth that would counteract the doctor's intervention? Why does life have to be so cruel? For the longest time, it did not seem possible that my mother would even have her own children, but to her utter amazement, she became pregnant. But on August 3, as quickly as she was rejoicing, the script changed to complete devastation.

In that moment, everything was focused on sight—not only the literal sight for a son but the vision a mom had of moving forward. Faced with the complete unknown and an impossible challenge, my mom had to fight every step of the way. While everything had created a complete blur, somehow there had to be a way forward.

Monday, August 8 kick-started a journey of medical attention that would be needed daily. Immediate intervention was provided on the operating table where the doctors feverishly worked to stabilize the extremely high pressures in my eyes. If I was going to have any chance of vision, those pressures needed to be addressed immediately. Thus, they sent me into emergency surgery at the Riley Children's Hospital under the direction of Dr. Forrest Ellis, a man my mom first met only hours before the surgery during an examination. Putting her infant's health into someone's hands is an absolute scary thought for any mother, but especially mine. Still, from the very first moment of meeting Dr. Ellis, my mom was moved by his gentleness and tremendous bedside manners. He made her comfortable with his care and plan for intervention, and the ability to salvage my eyes rested in the hands of the doctors inside the operating room.

On the fifth day, a mother dreams of having her first child at home, marveling at the possibilities for the future. On our fifth day, those possibilities were washed away in a blur of unwelcome circumstances.

Driving one way from my childhood home to the Riley Children's Hospital was approximately seventy miles; therefore, each round trip was a little under 150 miles. My mom logged thousands of miles just within the first year of my life. A week didn't go by that I didn't need to make a trip to Indianapolis for an evaluation or additional medical attention. Several of those weeks included multiple trips.

Here was a mother who had never traveled alone in a capital city and had never personally dealt with medical processes. Perseverance was—and is—a key element of my mom's character. Demonstrating grit, fighting all the way, my mom refused to give in to outside pressures. She sacrificed hours on the road, days in the doctor's office, and countless months meeting my needs at home.

Questioning her about those early years, I asked, "How did you ever get through it?"

Her response always includes determination and humor. She credited humor for lifting the ever-present stress in the situation, which provides some substance to "there is no better medicine than laughter." It's hard to envision my mom having time to laugh, though, for the outside pressures continually increased. Time did not offer hope, and her parents offered only opposition.

Unmovable in their devout faith, my mother's parents opposed medical action on my behalf. They believed God created me exactly the way he wanted. Should God want me to have vision, he would allow it. And if God intended for me to lose my sight, that was fine as well. Now I don't know if any of those feelings were derived from bitterness over my mom leaving or if they were completely formulated from their faith. What I do know is that the things they said to my mom were completely out of line. They called her a child abuser. Instead of supporting their daughter, they pointed fingers and blamed her for not being a fit parent. I could never understand how they could take a stance so strongly yet overlook the love that was needed. It was perfectly acceptable to cast their daughter and grandson to the side because their daughter wanted to give her son a fighting chance. Rather than making the picture of my mom's life a little clearer, they decided to make it harder. A sudden blur came from not only the monumental challenge of congenital glaucoma but also the loneliness in my mom's life. She had to fight, and she had to fight independently for her son.

Part of fighting independently for my mom was finding time to contemplate life's decisions and dig through her innermost thoughts through relaxing. As a child my mom would go to the churchyard to swing on the swing set. I think about her being a young girl, full of life, visualizing a bright future, fingers curled around the chains and moving her legs back and forth to create the swinging motion as the air whispered through her hair. It was a time far removed from the sudden blur she found herself in with me.

Life can look so different from one season to the next. Nobody truly knows what the future holds or how it will unfold. Never would that young girl have imagined her first son's eyesight swinging in the balance. Comfortably in the plastic swing, that little girl would clearly see the orchard, the church building, and all the property they resided on. Thoughts of blurred vision would have never crossed her mind. Despite being unprepared, pushing forward through the blur was the only option my mom had. Resiliency is the first word that comes to mind when I think about my mother. I admire her love, strength, and fortitude—her commitment to expend all of herself for one mission. The world would benefit immensely from hearing her message and receiving her teachings for other mothers who provide care for a disabled child.

During the coronavirus pandemic, I spent an extended amount of time with my mom in preparation for sharing my story. I asked her, "What would your advice be for other mothers and/or fathers who live with a child who has a disability?"

She told me that it is imperative you let them hurt, work through their emotions, and do not place them in a shell. Encourage your child to achieve, but also be transparent about the difficulties that await them. Many times, you are going to be compelled to be soft on your child, or you will be inclined to remove them from uncomfortable areas. Always remember, removing your child from tough situations does not truly prepare them for adulthood—or school days, for that matter.

My mom used to tell me, "Kurt you can be the president of the United States if you want to be." She did fear I would not be able to see her or that I would be bullied for my disability; however, playing second to all those emotions was her unwavering confidence that I could make something of myself. I can still hear my mom's voice from my teenage years telling me, "I'm not going to be around forever; you need to learn how to do these things." Mom never made excuses for my vision. She would take time to show me how to cook, do laundry, clean, garden, and any other home task you can think of.

From a child's perspective, I would add to her advice that while the days may be a blur, do not lose touch with each other. Work together as a team to overcome the disability.

Chapter 4

TREATMENT AND TRAJECTORY

Continuous care was needed for the first few months of my life. As Indiana fans closely monitor the scoreboard in the gym or the stopwatch at the Indianapolis Motor Speedway, so they carefully monitored the pressures in my eyes. Maintaining proper pressure inside my eyes would determine the long-term success of those early operations.

Dr. Ellis was truly a pioneer in the field of congenital glaucoma. Being born in 1988, the resources and research in this field were scarce for my care. Questions loomed about how much damage was done inside my mother's womb prior to birth and how much of my vision deterioration could be controlled. Dr. Ellis collaborated with fellow doctors across the country who charted congenital glaucoma cases; however, those cases were far and few between. Most studies pointed to adult cases.

On average, the human eyeball measures 24.2 millimeters by 23.7 millimeters. These measurements are based on an adult human and reflect the transverse diameter. For an infant, the average is even smaller—only 16.2 millimeters on average. Every cut and every procedure had to be precise to have any hope of success. Dr. Ellis spent weary nights and days trying to determine an appropriate path forward to provide the greatest results.

Dr. Forrest Ellis was born in Deputy, Indiana in the year 1932. He was accepted to the Indiana University School of Medicine where he discovered that he could be competitive in medicine. He also spent a year in the baseball program at Indiana and received a varsity letter sweater. The very next fall he stopped playing ball as his finances became tight. He recalls wearing the heavy letter sweater to football game days when he would walk up and down the aisles selling programs. I was amazed to discover that our paths both ran through Bloomington; we both carry the honor of being called Hoosiers and found athletics to be a very enjoyable portion of the college experience. After college, Dr. Ellis joined the 379th Bombardment Squadron, which was part of the strategic air command. Operating as a flight surgeon, Dr. Ellis credits his early interest in ophthalmology to his time spent in service.

After his time in service, Dr. Ellis started his journey in pediatric ophthalmology and was teamed up with the ophthalmology faculty at Indiana. Working at the time in the only childhood hospital in the state of Indiana, Dr. Ellis saw every case known to man at the Riley Hospital for Children. His peers often referred to him as a calm, compassionate, and solid guy. There were no books or manuals to instruct an order of operations for Dr. Ellis. Unfazed by the challenges, he worked in the areas of oculoplastic, DCRs, strabismus, cataract, glaucoma, and orbital work—truly a professional in the pediatric ophthalmology field, a man of all trades. Innovative is the only sufficient word when speaking about Dr. Ellis' tremendous career; he was labeled a pioneer in his field.

From his peers, fellows, and doctors, you would instantaneously learn that his character was admirable. Dr. Ellis had a special gift of putting children and parents at ease, and trust was established during the first visit. My mother echoes the same comments; she finds it hard to describe the level of care and superior bedside manners she experienced. Today Dr. Forrest Ellis is a member of the Pediatric Ophthalmology and Strabismus Hall of Fame.

On August 8, 1988, Dr. Ellis was assigned my case. With the sudden diagnosis of congenital glaucoma, my case was labeled as severe. I was immediately moved into an operating setting at the conjoining hospital. Providing treatment immediately gave my mom and the doctors hope for a positive trajectory in the days that would follow. Understanding that with each passing moment more damage was occurring in my optic nerve, the race was on to put a hold on the disease. If they could provide stability to the inner pressure of the eye, that could place a hold on future damage. The consensus amongst the doctors was that after the pressures were measured at an adequate level, regularly administered eye drops and monitoring would be the long-term path forward.

Today, I carry a small bag with me everywhere I travel that stores liquid gold. (If you assumed that meant Mountain Dew, you are mistaken, although that may be liquid silver to some). That liquid gold is small bottles of medication for inner eye pressure stabilization.

As I grew up, a focal point of in-person doctor visits was checking my eye pressure and looking at my optic nerve health. I can recall seeing and experiencing the transition and advancement in medicine during my appointments. I was one of the initial patients for what appeared to be an oversized permanent marker known as the Tono-Pen used to calculate eye pressure. Each time, a numbing drop was administered, and after a few seconds, Dr Ellis would gently hold my eyelid open and rub the rounded end against the surface of my eye. Hearing the clicks and a couple beeps as it registered, I would wiggle my toes in my shoes. I loved to hear the double beeps that meant a digital reading was displayed on the opposite end of the pen. Once my brother joined me at these appointments, we would relate our eye pressures to NASCAR driver numbers. Certainly there were only a handful of drivers you would catch between ten and twenty-two on normal visits. Neither of us were Tony Stewart fans at the time, and we would get upset if we happened to land on number twenty. And while I was a die-hard Jeff Gordon fan, landing the number twenty-four on the Tono-Pen was not a welcome reading from a medical standpoint. My brother's favorite car numbers were further out of reach as he rooted for the one and the ninety-seven.

This was a fun way to bond during our appointments. Dr Ellis would chuckle, and my mom would shake her head. Even though I came out the loser each time, we would still compete when checking visual acuity.

Over time, my vision continued to decline, and my eye pressures saw a greater range. No one knew or wanted to know how many times my head would rest on an operating table for surgery. The doctors put forth tireless efforts outside of the operating room to provide the best outcomes for my eyes. Those efforts included alterations in my drops and pressure patches, prescribing that my mom massage my eyes, and oral medications. The pursuit for somewhat normal vision became a battle to salvage just a portion of my sight.

I do not have the medical knowledge to understand or explain the intricate work that has occurred in my eyes; however, I do know that when an intern or resident student is granted permission to look into my eyes, they are astonished, and I get this feeling that my eyes are barely held together. They start exchanging all these fancy words and paying deep attention to my file, which is apparently remarkably interesting. I like to compare the experience to my childhood dalmatian, who would never break eye contact with me as I held a treat in my palm. There is always full eye contact and attention for several moments. Being the prized possession—or should I say prized patient? —does not always give you the warmest feelings, but over time I have adapted and learned to be welcoming to the doctors and aspiring physicians I meet.

Generally, the trajectory of my vision was believed to be positive after the bold early steps in my treatment. This thinking was not off base, but the sheer number of actions taken during the course of my treatment was unknown. Conditions such as calcium banding, cataracts, and scar tissue are all byproducts of excessive work, and these conditions can affect the overall health of the eye. Gradually I experienced a decline in my vision with these conditions. Calcium banding can be removed from the eye, but it will redevelop. The cataracts have been removed, and a new lens has been implanted. The scar tissue remains and cannot be changed.

There was a period of time during my later teen years when hope was rekindled for me to experience better vision with the removal of calcium and cataracts. The removal of both those things provided a temporary bump in my vision and, more importantly, a vivid display of color. I had never realized how vibrant and bold colors were until I got a glimpse of what was a new world for me. While the temporary bump faded back to the less vibrant colors, I was still thankful for the brief enhancement. Most importantly, my vision's trajectory has not led to complete blindness.

Blurred vision creates navigational obstacles, but it is still vision. Blindness in both eyes would have occurred if not for one crucial decision—a decision to break new ground, be innovative, and provide a first in the history of medicine. When I was growing up, Dr. Ellis came to a crossroads where sole responsibility for selecting the correct action rested on his shoulders. But would that action be sustainable for a young child?

Chapter 5

FIRST TO BALANCE
THE PRESSURE

As you may have already gleaned, glaucoma is caused by increased pressure in the eye. Having a glaucoma device implanted in the eye helps lower pressure by improving the way fluid drains from the eye.

In a healthy eye, a fluid called aqueous humor is made in the front of the eye and flows out through a tiny drain called the trabecular meshwork. The trabecular meshwork is in an area called the drainage angle. If fluid doesn't flow out of the drainage angle properly, eye pressure increases and will damage the optic nerve. Glaucoma implants help lower the pressure by increasing the flow of fluid out of the eye.

During glaucoma implant surgery, the drainage implant is usually placed underneath the upper or lower eyelid. Ophthalmologists will stitch the implant into the sclera (the white part of the eye). Ophthalmologists may also cover the tube of the implant with a patch fluid that will drain into the area around the implant. A tiny tube is attached to the drainage implant and inserted into the front chamber of the eye, usually just in front of the iris. The tube directs fluid from the inside of the eye to the implant, and from there it is absorbed into the body. Used to treat adult cases of glaucoma, these tube shunts had not been used in pediatrics for the treatment of congenital glaucoma at the time I was growing up.

Based on his analysis, and the understanding that progress was being lost when it came to balancing the pressure in my eyes (remember, uncontrolled pressures would mean additional damage and lower the likelihood of long-term sight), Dr. Ellis stepped into a new medical area and performed operations during which he installed Molteno tubes in both my right and left eye. The surgeries were successful, but factors of growth could only be measured by time.

Since I was only five years old at the time, full development was still off in the distance, and close monitoring would be necessary to ensure the tubes did not move or close. Any changes would require additional visits to the operating room to ensure the fluid was draining as it should. The greatest testament to the work that was completed when I was age five is the fact that I have never had to have my tubes replaced or repositioned. This is quite remarkable considering that I was the first pediatric patient to receive this treatment. Dr.

Ellis used his precision and knowledge of future medicine first on me.

I have often pondered what my life would have looked like had I been born five to ten years earlier. The result would likely be me living in darkness, living a life in blindness. But this very contemplation has been a cause for rejoicing. Yes, damage was done, the limitation is still there, but I was granted a chance to experience this life with a sliver of sight. The numbers pointed toward extremely limited vision but later would demonstrate that a stand was being created for God's glory.

Glaucoma is a progressive optic neuropathy and is the leading cause of irreversible blindness and the second most common cause of blindness worldwide. There is no way to predict the future or lay out a road map for personal sight and duration of that sight after the diagnosis. Every three months, an evaluation is conducted to monitor any such changes in the eyes.

Knowing that losing additional vision is a real possibility, or even complete blindness, is an extremely terrifying reality to live with. While it's extremely limited in nature, I still cherish the vision I do have and want to hold onto it until the moment I take my last breath. Yet, at the time of authoring this book, I am thirty-three years old and count myself blessed to have reached this phase of my life with my limited sight intact. The pressure associated with the eyes and life does have a unique correlation. Vision truly is in a position to create beautiful imagery and open a space to speak truth. I highlighted a first in the journey to balance eye pressure in a pediatric glaucoma patient, but this is also the beginning of a wonderfully designed path to push access to the gospel forward.

Courage to push into the unknown, to work in such a delicate and fragile space, is remarkable, especially creating a tiny space for a tube to maintain the health of the eye and provide a solution to stop the damage and enable sight. It is unbearable for me to think about the point of decision for Dr. Ellis and having the presence of mind to make a critical decision that would directly affect someone's future. Pressure was on the rise in my eye, but it did not affect his steady hand in surgery. No matter how tedious, action was taken on my behalf. And today, I celebrate the success of the first life-altering surgery on a birth defect, and I am forever thankful for the provision that was made and balance that was reached.

Chapter 6

SIGHTS AND SOUNDS

Preparations for an additional eye surgery had begun at the Riley Children's Hospital in Indianapolis. I vividly remember the day I was scheduled to have surgery. I loved how they would always prepare a wagon to take kids back to the operating room, making it so cozy with warm blankets and a pillow. Although it was a fun ride, it was also scary to leave my mom and go into the unknown. There would always come a point when my mom would fade off into the distance, whether that was leaving the preparation room or headed behind the double doors.

Entering the large operating room, I still can remember the blue walls and the chill in the air. Being lifted onto the operating table always caused me anxiety and triggered a defensive reflex so that I felt like I needed to be on guard. My eyes were instantly scanning for the gas mask that they would use to put me to sleep. The anesthesiologist would ask me what flavor I wanted added to the gas mask, and I honestly believe this is the origin for my dislike of grape flavor today. You will never win me over with a grape-flavored Tootsie Pop. It is always a 100 percent safe bet that those will be left in the bag.

Fighting to not go to sleep before an operation, I would become outraged with the doctors. My mom said that I would throw a fit and oftentimes try to bite the medical assistants. This escalated to the point that my mom was asked to gown up and come into the operating room. As they placed the mask on my face, they would softly say, "Kurt, you are going to go to the moon."

I would reply that I did not want to go to the moon.

My mom hated to see the tears running down my face, but she wanted to make me as comfortable as possible. There was even one time when she put the mask up to her face for a moment, but the anesthesiologist warned her not to do that. I can only imagine what my reaction would have been if Mom had breathed in too much of the gas.

After I stopped fighting them, they would place the mask on my face and hold it firmly, and I would become drowsy while breathing in the gassy grape fumes. I hated the feel of the rubber seal around my face, the awful smell, and the feeling of dropping away. I remember thinking I would never let it happen again. For future operations, I did request not to use the gas mask. Typically, for younger children, they use a gas mask instead of running an IV at the start. The nurses were so accommodating even with the IV as they would numb the back of my hand with some cream. Overlaying the cream with a clear bandage, they would use a marker to draw a smiley face. In my opinion, the needle was a far better option than the gas mask. After multiple surgeries, I started to enjoy having conversations with the nurses and learning each step that was involved leading up to an operation. I could always bribe them for an extra warm blanket in the operating room. But I kept my promise to myself, and I never heard "let's make a trip to the moon" before going to sleep again.

Despite the surgeries, light sensitivity continues to be a real issue that I deal with on a continual basis. Several pictures during my youth show me with an eye patch taped to my face. As much as I did not like the uncomfortable nature of the patch, I did like the darkness it would create. Even during the times when a patch was not taped over either eye, I would still squeeze my eyes shut to provide some relief from the light.

Throughout the day, my mom would desperately try to get me to open my eyes and keep them open. Wondering if she would ever get me to open my eyes, she tried to devise creative ways to make me want to keep them open. Whether it was pulling the shades in the house or creating a dimly lit room, she worked to create a darker environment for me. Success always came after sunset when my mom would pick me up and open the door so we could walk out into the yard. Talking about the night sky, my mom would gently open my eyes and say, "Light." The stars would be shining, and the moon would be illuminated from the reflective light of the sun. My little eyelids would slowly begin to open on their own and admire the night sky. Many precious nights were spent in my mom's arms as she continued to talk to me about the light. It was exciting to later learn that my second spoken word was "light." For the longest time, the only light I knew came from the night sky, in particular the moon. It did not matter to me where the light was coming from; all that mattered was that the light at night was easier on my sensitive eyes. I give credit to my mom for being creative and working with me to make sure I enjoyed my sight.

My development was always at the forefront of my mom's mind. As she would clean the house, she would talk to me in my carrier. Eventually, I began to wiggle and turn my head in her direction, and she could see the signs of intelligence and cleverness in her son. Of course, fears loomed in her mind about what school would look like for me and how other kids might respond, which was a large reason for her focus on my development.

Often attributed to a gift from God, my communication has always been strong. My mom may not want to wear the crown of credit, but I genuinely believe her dedication to development also played a crucial role in my gift of communication. Spending exorbitant amounts of time in the local library, she would sign onto a computer to conduct research not only on my condition but also on developmental processes. One example was that she learned to take photos at the zoo of the animals that were in the distance or were too small for me to recognize. Taking these small, but important, measures expanded my thinking and bettered my interactions with my environment.

Riding in the back seat of the old Ford Thunderbird, we would head with my mom to New Castle or Muncie to do the shopping. And when I say "we," I'm including my favorite white teddy bear that I would never leave at home. I always found it comforting to be riding in the car and listening to old cassette tapes playing. Never dreaming of leaving my mom's side, I would begin to correspond with people around me as we were doing the shopping (well, at least when I wasn't chewing on the Cool Whip container). Unbelievably, I can remember rolling through the Ross grocery store as my mom would shop. I would hear the clatter of the grocery carts and the voices mixing across the aisles. All the while I was just waiting for Dire Straits to play on the speaker system. Loving the beat and background music to "Walk of Life," I remember always swinging my feet.

At our usual grocery story, I befriended a woman named Dolly once when we were rolling through the checkout line, and I always requested afterward that we went through her line. I'm sure there were times when my mom waited extra long just to ensure that I could see Dolly. The distraction of a circus wagon animal cracker box might grab my attention for a moment, but I always enjoyed hearing from Dolly the most.

Pulling out of the grocery store parking lot, our next stop would be Gomel's Meat Market. Unlike Dolly, I did not know any of the gentleman's names behind the meat counter. What I did realize was that there was a glass jar resting on the countertop filled with mini suckers. I hoped that I would be offered a sucker at the end of the packaging if I showed complete interest in their work. Overall, it was a rather good deal. I would get a sucker, and later I would enjoy a famous A1 steak burger.

Really what it came down to was that I took an interest in different people around me. I was curious to see what they were doing and what they would say. Fascinated with different voices and sounds, I absorbed all that I could. Perhaps because I rely on my senses other than sight, I have been said to remember too much detail. Clearly I was not carrying around a notepad in those early years, and I can say that I still do not carry one today. It is never a point of effort for me to remember things; remembering naturally occurs in my mind.

(Of course, I realize there needs to be caution when talking about my memory bank. When I consider a future spouse, I suppose a strong memory could set me up for a hard escape. I know I will have to play my cards right, and the blurry vision just might have to be my get-out-of-jail-free card.)

I continue to learn by holding pages close or a screen a couple inches from my face; however, there is no other mechanism that contributes more to my learning than sound. Reaping the benefits from this style of learning, I have become more detailed in my interactions. It helped me build a foundation for excellence in customer service, sales, and directing athletic tours that I do today. I fully believe that a disability creates an ability. Employers should give special consideration to those who live with a disability. Exploratory questions can lead them to see that individuals who have a disability also have a unique capability to enhance the workplace, and it gives employers a chance to serve alongside the most loyal individuals in the workforce.

Through my nearsightedness and an abundance of auditory input, my growth is continual. I strive to be the best individual I can while also being the best team player I can. Sights and sounds became key identifiers for not only victory in work but also victory in life.

Chapter 7

LIFE CAN'T BE
MARSHMALLOWS AND RAISINS

One of the best ways to remember things you learn is to attach those items to a story. Taking in content and stories that stick in our memory enables us to not only appreciate but grow in knowledge and understanding. In my role as an author and teacher, I commit myself to thinking thoroughly through how I can best connect with an audience. Hopefully receiving this insight early in the book will make it easy to understand my viewpoint, although let's hope that is not the only sticking point from this book.

Considering my story about how my mom helped me discover light in the night, often the night indicates family time.

My guess is that popcorn is the most sought-after snack when it comes to family time and enjoying a movie together. But have you ever filled the popcorn bowl with marshmallows and raisins? Have you ever thought about that combination for a snack? You see, my personal favorite snack during my youth was marshmallows with raisins. Sitting on top of an upside-down laundry basket, I would have a bowl of marshmallows and raisins. Consuming space on the kitchen floor as my mom worked, I would have a bowl of marshmallows and raisins. I've thought about investigating packaging them together and selling the combination as an official snack on your local grocery store shelves. It could quite literally change the snacking game throughout every household, although that might be a bit overboard since I don't think popcorn is going to be pushed aside or ice cream will be left behind to develop freezer burn. Still, I am telling you that marshmallows and raisins are the perfect snack.

Knowing that this combination is my favorite snack, I want to instill the lesson that life cannot be a bowl of marshmallows and raisins. Indeed, I liked the flavor, but I also liked the obvious contrast between the two different foods with the marshmallow being white and the raisin almost appearing black. Anyone who is visually impaired will tell you that sharp contrast is a terrific thing. For example, using yellow stripes on the edge of stairs or using a black background on your computer screen creates higher contrast. Marshmallows and raisins happen to be black and white, making it easy for me to identify the elements in the bowl. But life cannot be a series of black and white events.

Frankly, I do not think that anyone wants all things to be black and white visually; people want black and white in areas in which they need direction. Color is desired visually, but we can all think of times when we wished everything could be crystal clear. Decisions regarding finances, family matters, or a career change can be pivotal moments, let alone receiving news from the doctor that you must make a critical health decision. In cases such like those, it would be nice to have a card in our pocket that read, "Let's keep it black and white." You could pull out that card and it would automatically give you the best possible outcome with only one right and one wrong outcome to choose from. Yet, it would take away the need for faith and dependence. We would be as powerful as God.

When I ask my mom what her single biggest fear was during my early years, without hesitation, she responds, "It was a worry about whether you would be able to see my face and recognize me as your mom." She could not come to terms with the thought that her son might not be able to see or recognize her face, never knowing his mom's appearance or seeing her smile. That fear weighed heavy on her heart. She desperately wanted her baby boy to see the care and love she held for him.

After my initial surgeries, she knew that a portion of my sight had been salvaged. While she wanted to be thankful, she remained hesitant, worried that future changes as I developed could cause a complete loss of sight. Writing this at the age of thirty-two, I can claim that I know my mom by sight. Eventually my mom did reach a point when she understood that I recognized her face and that wonderful smile, but there were several years when my mom was in a difficult place. It was not black and white for me to maintain just a sliver of vision.

The expectation was set early on that I would only need a few surgeries on my eyes. The prognosis was extremely concerning, but the outlook remained positive. Dr. Ellis performed extraordinary work. His knowledge and expertise were expansive and well-regarded across the country. To the best of his knowledge based on his calculations and understanding, he did believe that only four to five operations would be necessary to stabilize my eye pressures and preserve near normal vision. He's told me that my case would keep him up at night, and he would often share my portfolio with other glaucoma specialists. I know that my case was never a black and white matter for him personally; he maximized my care to provide the absolute best results. At the most recent count, I have undergone forty eye operations, far surpassing the original estimate of four to five. No one could have guessed that forty surgeries would be performed. If they had known that number at the beginning, neither of them would have been thrilled at the thought. They would have only been left with doubt and worry about how much vision I would be able to enjoy. With the numbers never black and white, they both continued to push forward fighting for a better tomorrow. Even though all I see now are blurry objects, thank goodness I can still see through blurred vision.

Caught in the middle of so many unknowns as I grew up persisted the perplexing theme: what would the future look like? Parents want their kids to have a fulfilling life and prosper beyond what they personally experienced. Starting with a setback only twenty-four hours into my life and discovering on the fifth day that emergency surgery was needed disintegrated my mom's hope for a prosperous future. As uncomfortable as the waiting room chair in the hospital was, so was my mother's outlook. Never having stepped foot in a medical complex nor encountering medicine, my mom was at a tipping point with her first son. The ultimate test that proved there would be no signs of life being black and white was found in my early days. No one could provide a clear answer on what my future would entail—this physical condition that would directly impact every aspect of my future. To the letter, my sight was in the balance. It was possible that things would work out, but was it probable? My mom had to take a turn away from meaning into management of my young life. A future with action steps would need to be ordered in a far different manner than fellow children.

I hope you understand why marshmallows and raisins symbolize far more in my journey than just high-contrast colors. It is easy for someone to offer advice not to get discouraged about the unknowns, but they do not understand the other person's situation. When faced with that truth, people often follow with the generic response: "Things will work out and I will uplift you in my prayers." While this is a very generic response, the fact of the matter is that things can work out and prayer *will* make all the difference. Through my testimony and ever-changing process, I hope you can see that things were rarely black and white in my early days, but my blurred vision brought me one of the most amazing blessings on this side of heaven. Eventually my message and purpose

Chapter 8

WHERE PRESENT
MEETS PREPARATION

A ccepting my limited vision helped my mom and care team deliver prompt action steps for a redesigned approach to childhood. Like a carpentry job, tools were necessary to build not only a functional framework, but a stable foundation. My mom proactively sought assistance to guide me through academics and help me learn life skills, undeterred by the reality that tools were necessary but would need to be different than they were for other children.

I applaud my mother for refusing to make excuses and being proactive in her pursuit to find assistance. She would travel several miles to spend time in the library computer lab doing independent research and scrolling for help. This was before most homes had a personal computer, smartphone, or tablet. When I think about my mother's willingness to extend herself and provide the best chance for her son, I could fill a chalkboard with incredible adjectives to describe my mother's amazing ability to lead, "proactive" being the first to appear.

My mom quickly pushed her mind into preparation rather than pity. Her self-awareness in understanding her need for help led her to search for a low-vision aid in our region. I was paired with the identified aid for fourteen years, walking in stride through every academic year. The weight of my diagnosis was felt with every report card, but the inked letters were the smallest indicators of the greater lessons. The weight of my developmental process came from the wait; repetition and patience were necessary for my development. The tools had to be molded to fit my hands, and my blueprint had to be personalized.

Professionally, I place being proactive and dedicated as imperative qualities for assembling positive outcomes. These two qualities applied from my mother and low-vision aid are purposely mirrored in my life, and I attribute my personal success to their implementation. They gave me guidance and taught me mannerisms that pushed me in a direction I would not have chosen on my own.

Have you ever heard the statement: "Today's choices create tomorrow's outcomes"? This simple, but absolutely true, statement applies to every walk of life. People will inherently choose the easiest path forward, oftentimes the path with the least amount of work involved. I can remember times when my low-vision aid would go with me to school a week before classes started to help me find my locker and walk me through my entire class schedule to familiarize me with the locations and the paths I would need to take. One of the more difficult tasks visually was reading the dial on my lock to my locker. Not wanting to look different by hovering my eyes only a couple inches away from the digits, I would leave the combination in place to keep the locker door unlocked. I prepared the door for easy access, accepting that it could be accessed by anyone. I had prepared the door once, but I did not prepare each day, all the while risking theft. Committing to the future today means participating in preparation daily. Unlike my locker approach, we should not take one day to prepare and depend upon it to carry us through the rest. Time is a gift; that is why they call it the present. What are you going to do with the present?

Knowing my mother's background and the extent to which my diagnosis was unfamiliar territory for her, waiting instead of preparing would have been 100 percent within the bounds of acceptability for her actions. It would have been much easier for her to take the sympathetic approach and accept that my life would just be different. But embodying a relentless spirit and grit, my mom pushed forward and capitalized on the present.

Indeed, things were going to be different, but that did not change the amount of preparation she conducted. The only thing that changed was the plan, a plan that would support the visually impaired. When I ask my mom questions about the early days and transitioning me into school, she credits getting through the tough times partially to using humor but also, most of all, to being open to instruction and advice from Dr. Ellis and my low-vision aid. Motherly instincts do kick in, of course, but I am continually impressed with the amount of perseverance my mom demonstrated during these years. There was no delay. Instead, her mind was focused on complete preparation. I have so much admiration for the overwhelming amount of love and fight she demonstrated. I live today with the understanding that the present is meant for preparation. That understanding is deeply rooted in who I am because of the woman who raised me.

Instant gratification has run rampant throughout society in today's operations. In fact, I like to call it a microwave society. How many times does somebody get upset when they think the microwave takes too long? Impatience starts to creep in when we have not heard a response from a text message in ten minutes. We want the reward or pat on the back before the accomplishment. Online platforms have accelerated a generation of people who want to share everything, and if it does not have ten likes in the first ten minutes, something is wrong. There is a purpose in the preparation; promotion does not occur in the present. It is not a curse to be separated from others for a time, to work quietly and prepare without the noise. Through a combination of choice and circumstance, I have lived a life marked by singleness throughout my teens and twenties. I find it amazing that many people deem this to be a lonely state of living. My choices do not mean that I do not want to share my life with someone here on earth, but through the separation and preparation, I was becoming a man fit to love his future wife as he should. I am thankful for the time of discovery, self-reflection, and building long-lasting friendships.

Gazing into the past with active tear ducts each day was once my present reality. Those days didn't bolster hope, have a peak of promise, or offer gratitude, yet the present day was not tossed aside. Most individuals who God has aligned with my life do not fear the amount of exertion a day takes but fear a day where they are not fighting for something greater. There were a multitude of days that were a difficult fight, but there remained a relentless dedication to service. What was poured out was black and white, but everything else was blurred.

One of the things I most often ask myself is: what is black and white to me? On Mondays, the world says, "we need extra coffee" or "it's okay to have a bad attitude," and I'd chose in the present that was not what I was going to pour out. For what is black and white is a love for those around me, a love that reflects the One who is the light of my life and who has granted me the fullness of life eternal. Preparation means pouring love to my classmates, my coworkers, my teammates, my community, my generation, and the world. The years we are granted are a precious gift and a remarkable opportunity to leave a mark of service rather than a mark of status—a present that is matched with purpose and a message that points to an eternal future with the creator of the universe.

So, maintain an attitude of being willing to respond in the present rather than waiting to feel something new. When we succumb to acting upon our emotions, we are tossed about like a ship at sea. The waves of emotions that have covered my head are far too many to count. Waking up and not being able to change my visual impairment offers an abundance of feelings. Every single person is going to live through an abundance of emotions—the highs, the lows, and the in-betweens. Planning to act when alignment and comfortability mesh is a recipe for a life lost at sea.

Write the following phrase on a notecard and place it somewhere you can see it: Feelings turn you, but faith moves you forward.

To engage in preparation is to be present, assuming accountability for the day you have been granted. It is about having awareness and not being displaced by anxiety. It is understanding that through Christ, we are enough. It's living with a purpose to pursue the King of Glory. Ultimately, we determine what we are going to act upon and how we are going to present ourselves each day. Choose to turn opposition into opportunities with a persevering mentality. Feed your mind with confidence and relish in the comfort that a strong mind wins over feelings—a mind that is focused on a plan, a mind that understands what is greater, and a mind that sees alternative perspectives.

Through Blurred Vision boldly brings life forward, uncovering the vulnerabilities and firsthand experience of someone with low vision, but everyone has their version of low vision. Steps taken in the present and in preparation have opened the door for a unique way to share love, hope, and a game plan for higher living. I hope you discover in these pages complete peace for the journey that has been assigned to you and a purpose that holds eternal value.

Chapter 9

A BROTHER IS FOR ADVERSITY

A friend loveth at all times,
and a brother is born for adversity
—Proverbs 17:17

W hile my mom's preparation was instrumental, a lifetime partner was needed. Gladness lives inside of each day knowing I was given a best friend. Referring to Proverbs 17:17, you notice that a brother is born for adversity. Those words could easily be taken out of context, especially with the heading of this chapter. In the verse, a brother is a fellow Christian. Well, my literal brother has demonstrated nothing but love and care toward me, and he is a fellow believer. I have established multiple meaning-ful friendships, several I would classify as best friends, but above all my brother is truly my partner and my stronghold. He's been there almost every step of the way with me, and I only say almost because there's a few years of separation between us. Years might highlight that separation, but there is no separation to be found in our friendship. With no scientific reason, only a God-given design, my brother has been part-nered with me in both love and adversity. I have a Father who is in heaven and a brother who walks in similar shoes with me. Not forgotten nor left alone, our blueprint was created with our relationship in full focus. The plan was prepared, and clear knowledge of this purpose provides a shared apprecia-tion in our brotherly bond.

In the months leading up to my brother's arrival, the word "sister" was stuck in my vocabulary. I had it set in my mind that I wished to welcome a baby sister into the world. Thank-fully not all wishes become reality. Four and half years after my entrance into the world, my younger brother came forth with a glowing complexion and gorgeous eyes. At least, that is certainly what everyone had to say about my new baby brother. Those were not exactly my thoughts and words, but I certainly was pleased to hold him.

You see, our relationship started off as rivals when I began to see my brother as superior to me. Today it breaks my heart to remember some of the anger that I had toward my brother at a young age. It was my understanding that his vision was normal and mine was far less than normal, and that made me frus-trated. Tussling on the living room floor, I remember saying,

"You need to stop, or I will poke your eyes out." Bitterness would erupt in times of discontent, and I would exclaim, "How would you like to not see?"

Those feelings still did not change for a couple of years. The transition finally was initiated when we discovered the value in each other's strengths. I became a voice for my brother, and he became my eyes. Slowly there was a progression from rivals to comradery. One of the funnier times this came in handy was during the summer months when our mom would leave us money to order a pizza for delivery. My brother refused to call in the pizza order, so I would pick up the phone to call in the order. Fast-forwarding to today, our strengths still hold true. My professional career heavily involves people and my brother's involves working with equipment. While I am most comfortable in a group setting, my brother is most comfortable in a tree stand or in the Rocky Mountains hunting on his own.

With our differences in desires and approaches, our bond became strong through family dysfunction and divorce. We were the ones who had to honor visitation rights and experience split holidays. Knowing the hardships, we partnered to make the best out of an unpleasant situation. Deprived of support from our biological father and experiencing the falling away of our stepdad, we learned to lean on each other. That bond in our partnership and support created an unbreakable link. It is easy to tear one piece of paper, but as the pages are added, it becomes increasingly harder to tear apart. This is true in our lives. A lot was stacked on us, but it made us so we could not be torn apart.

Going back to our childhood, my brother started complaining of pain and rubbing his eyes at age three and was scheduled for an examination. After gathering some items in a bag for entertainment purposes, we left the house anticipating a long day. The day had arrived for my brother to be tested for congenital glaucoma. I remember sitting in front of a vent in the waiting room where clicking noises would take place on a rather frequent basis through the long wait. I would gaze in the direction they took my brother to see if I could pick up any movement. The doctors had stated that my brother was being a challenge, and my mom always said that my brother was going to cause her trouble (a sincere joke as my brother has played a crucial role in my mom's life today). That day, the challenge was sedating my brother for the examination. He simply would not go to sleep while I was growing anxious outside.

After the examination, I remember being called back to the room with my dad. Passing through the doorway, my mom was leaning over my brother as he lay still on the table. Advancing a few more steps, I could feel her tears, hear the sorrow that was springing forth. Remaining a couple steps behind her, I clutched the bag of entertainment that was in my hand, standing still, listening as the difficult prognosis of congenital glaucoma was relayed by my mom. Feeling horrible, I slouched my shoulders in disbelief; I couldn't bear the thought that my brother had been given the same medical prognosis as myself. Enough time had lapsed that we thought everything was normal, and there were no concerns connected to my brother's vision. Yet, in this moment, the bottom fell out, a distraught mother headed right down the same road again. Joining the 0.0001 percent, my brother also carried the label of congenital glaucoma.

Dr. Ellis also performed surgery on my brother to install Molteno tubes, just as he had for me. The driving fear was congenital glaucoma, but my brother's vision was far stronger than mine. In my case, a lot of the damage occurred pre-birth and through multiple surgeries. The surgeries provided a lifeline, but the scar tissue increased with each operation. Weighing the outcome of no sight against no action, it was worth the risk even knowing there would be side effects, and they remained hopeful in my brother's case that he would have normal sight if his pressures were stabilized in a timely manner. Completing the necessary operations, his pressures were brought to a normal level. Regularly scheduled visits would be needed as eye drops were prescribed, and there were many times my brother would be with me during office checkups.

For all the times I was thankful that my brother was with me in the examination chair, I am especially grateful for his presence during adversity. I could not have moved forward without him in times of extreme adversity. It's an absolute shame that the most difficult people in our lives have been our dad and our stepfather. Each of the two circumstances carries different challenges but the same heartache.

During my teen years, I used my voice to go in a separate direction from my father. Struggling later with thoughts of my selfishness and immaturity, I regret leaving my brother behind when I did so. I was so hurt and uncomfortable around my father that I simply wanted to get away, but my brother had to continue with visitation on his own because of his age. There were a couple of weekends when I rejoined my dad and brother for visits, and those times would yield the same result where I did not want to continue visiting my dad. During one intense argument in the car, my dad stopped at the local store to pick up milk and soda. Both my brother and I refused to join him in the store to pick up these items. Distraught and discontent after the argument, I wanted to drive away and asked my brother in the back seat if he felt comfortable being my eyes as I drove back to New Castle. With no driver's license and limited sight, I was on the brink of leaving my dad behind at the store and going home. My brother was slightly hesitant, but he agreed to come up to the front seat. Recalling the way my blood was boiling, it had to be fear that kept me from leaving that parking lot—not a fear of driving on the road but fear of what would happen once my dad had discovered we left.

Looking in the rearview mirror, I was upset knowing that my brother had faced a lot of grim times alone. Without a doubt I know that tough conversations and arguments took place when I was not present. This is where I give credit to my brother's strength, which was greater than mine. In fact, he endured a lot of tough things that I stepped away from. Our relationship is stronger than ever, but I wish I could take back the times when I left him behind to deal with my dad alone.

During my college years, it was like wash and repeat through the same darn mess. I would stay in close communication with my brother, but he was left to deal with my stepfather's anger. The timing worked out that college pulled me out of the most challenging years of living with my stepfather. The verbal abuse that my mom and brother received daily was unbelievable. Peace at home was absent but delivering a piece of his mind was an everyday occurrence. Building calluses for his emotions, my brother would go toe-to-toe with my stepdad in arguments, including physical contact. It truly became a fight for power, and my mom was left trying to be a mediator. With only the few words that my brother provides, I still do not know about all the interactions that arose during my absence. I do know that my brother decided to move forward and not elaborate about the oppressive times he faced. Speaking only for myself, the relationship struggles with both my dad and my stepfather have made a lasting impact. I would relate them to a scar; they fade over time but never truly fade away.

Approaching God and asking for forgiveness not only for ourselves but for our dad and our stepfather allows us to move forward. I pray the lessons we have learned will shape us into phenomenal husbands, fathers, and leaders in the home. I hope that our pain will lead to a blessed future for our wives and kids. Our lives suffered a delay connected to marriage, but I know that delay has a purpose, trusting and believing that exciting days are ahead for my brother and I as life unfolds.

Always looking out for each other, it thrills us to look back on how my brother has helped me. There is no better example than the winter mornings going to school. Heading down our eighth-of-a-mile-long driveway, my brother would always lead the way. The darkness in the morning made it hard for me to see the potholes or mud puddles scattered throughout the gravel. There would be a soft orange glow in the sky from the distant town center, but for me it didn't make a difference. My brother would lead the way and help me avoid all the trouble areas along the driveway. When we had to wait at the end of the driveway, I would talk to my brother about NASCAR or some sporting event. Even though he probably was not completely listening, he would bear with me and these types of conversations. He could have easily been aggravated or tired of hearing me talk, but he still always helped me as we stepped onto the bus. He would also lead the way down the aisle in between the bus seats. I had been known to sit on a fellow kid's sleeping head because I thought the seat was open in the darkness. A few steps ahead, my brother would identify an open seat on the bus and slap the backrest so that I could hear where I should sit. Without his guidance, I would have been stressed and anxious going through the process alone. With his vision to help me, I was so thankful that this portion of my daily journey was smoother. Pulling words together may not be my brother's strong suit, but he has a heart of gold and he looks out not only for me but for all those close to him.

While the care between us always existed, so did the competitive side of our relationship. There were multiple times when my brother would push me to new heights—or into new trees. Behind our house in New Castle was a small hill that ran along our backyard. Placing the rear wheels of our bicycles against the cement patio, we would race down the hill toward the garden. Located just west of the garden was a tree stump we had marked as the finish line. During one of these races, our bikes got hooked together as we sped side by side down the hill into the final stretch. Somehow while remaining upright himself, my brother kicked my bike loose, and I veered left into the pine trees. Thank goodness the pine trees were soft. Instead of going to victory lane, I was wearing tree sap.

I would rarely bow down from a competition. Even though the doctors banned baseball with a pitcher for me, I wasn't afraid to face my brother's fastball in the backyard until the day he delivered a jam shot to the hands and I came out with a bloody thumb. Like a sponge, I would watch my brother and soak up as much knowledge as I could. I did not want to be left behind, and I also wanted to evaluate how things were done. My greatest teacher for many life skills and talents was my younger brother, and our competitiveness produced a better version of me.

Now, holidays are times when I like to take an interest in my brother's activities. Near and dear to my brother's heart is hunting. Personally, I enjoy fishing the most, but I have found it enjoyable to spend time with my brother in the woods. I have a certain set of skills (listening and hearing) that make me excellent for the hunt! Shouldn't this be the perfect setup for identifying deer? Sitting in the deer blind, my ears are always on high alert. I will gently nudge my brother's elbow, pointing in the direction where I believe a deer will come from, and ask, "Did you hear that?"

His short response is usually, "No, that's squirrels."

I mutter to myself, "Sure are noisy little guys." I proceed to pull my cell phone out to take a video of the bushy tails scrambling for food a few feet from the hunting blind. Later I usually hear more commotion and tell my brother I hear something moving. This time he responds, "You are hearing birds."

Maybe my hearing isn't the sharp skill my brother needs in the woods ... I never realized the woods could be so noisy once you settle in and become silent. Nevertheless, this once again points to the countless times my brother created special experiences for me. As adults, those creative times have not stopped, and we have experienced endless laughs and enjoyable times, even at my expense. (Yes, I still know that you received extra credit in high school by telling one of these stories, brother.)

God in his ultimate wisdom knew I needed a younger brother. He gave me a best friend who experiences congenital glaucoma right along with me, but his is designed differently with normal vision. It is a miracle because my mom was not expecting to have kids, and then my brother was given the 0.0001 percent diagnosis as well. The entire process can only be explained by a loving and all-knowing God.

My brother has faced his own challenges and questions about why things must be the way they are. In times of frustration, he has said, "Maybe my life purpose is just to help you." This is not entirely true, because I know God has a great purpose for my brother's life unattached from mine. However, if this was the only one thing that was my brother's purpose in life, he's done it to perfection. I give God all the glory for providing me with a brother for a life of adversity. On my work desk is a picture of me and my brother that my brother gave me as a Christmas gift. The frame reads: "started as brothers, became best friends." That perfectly represents our relationship, and I love him for the man and friend he is today.

Chapter 10

ANGRY AT GAME TIME

P rior to enjoying NASCAR, basketball, and football, baseball was my selected sport. As a young boy living in the state of Indiana, I can remember watching the Cincinnati Reds on television. Of course, those were the good old days when Indiana was in the central time zone. That meant our antenna would pick up the Dayton, Ohio station and the Reds' games would start at 6 p.m. It is amazing to think back to those days and then look at today and see how fast time has flown by. Sometimes I play with the idea that I am getting old, but I was not old enough to witness The Big Red Machine. Nevertheless, I thoroughly enjoyed watching the Reds play baseball. I mean, I thought *Wheel of Fortune* was cool for a few minutes, but I would much rather watch baseball. In the house, in the backyard, and even in my collector's book, you can see evidence of my appetite for the game of baseball.

Without shame, I still turn the volume up during "Centerfield" by John Fogerty—an absolute classic that has been enjoyed by millions. Since 1985, "Centerfield" has been played throughout the country at all levels of baseball over the speakers of hundreds of ballparks. But while I may have been clapping to the song, my intentions were quite different than simply singing along. My version would go like this: "Oh mom forced me in the game, I'm not ready to play today!"

At the time I made up that rendition, my mother made the decision to sign me up for the local tee-ball league. Completely appalled by the decision, I claimed that I could not participate. A baseball field was the last place I wanted to be. I felt much more comfortable outside the fences, away from the field of play. I found comfort not in public but rather in independent living away from the noise of life. Fear penetrated my mind when I thought about not being able to see the faces in the grandstands. I was afraid I would be embarrassed that I could not always see the baseball.

That fear quickly turned into anger that my mom had put me in a no-win situation. Granted, it was only tee-ball, but at the time, it seemed like a whole new world. It was a position that I did not want to be in, completely pushed outside of my comfort zone. No amount of coaxing or convincing could turn my mind away from the devastating imagery.

I expected to always be positioned in the dugout and would not have blamed anyone for saying I was destined to be best friends with the water cooler at the end of the bench. Choosing to endure and outlast the challenging times seems to be a common response when people are faced with a moment of discomfort. Both my mother and my tee-ball coach acknowledged that I was outside of my comfort zone, and I was quite literally green behind the ears. "Rookie" was not an adequate description of my status coming into baseball. Yet, those two wonderful individuals did not give up and decided to invest in me.

Putting on the baseball cap, jersey t-shirt, and white baseball pants, I looked the part but certainly did not feel the part. What would happen when I stepped onto the field? Surely I was destined to embarrass myself and my team. And I was only thinking in the context of practice, not even thinking about a game-time situation. I was completely out of my element when it came to beginning the game of baseball. But all this never discouraged my baseball coach from spending time with me not only in practice but also in additional time after practice. I learned how to place my hands on the baseball bat, hold my position at the plate, and take note of my feet as I was swinging. I had my fair share of mishaps when I would swing above the ball, knock the tee-ball stand over, and even lose my helmet as I fell. I stumbled and fell outside of my comfort zone on a regular basis. In fact, it seemed like the struggle ran on a repeated schedule.

While it may sound like being outside my comfort zone was a traumatic experience for me, one of my most powerful life lessons came when I operated outside of my comfort zone. When was the last time you operated outside of your comfort zone? What was your response to an adverse environment? Was there a greater lesson waiting to be unveiled?

Growing in confidence, I finally began to find my footing in the batter's box. Ultimately, I decided the tee-ball stand was hindering my ability to hit the ball. I began requesting the pitching machine not only in practice but also during game time at-bats. My mindset had totally taken a 180-degree turn. Soon I could not wait to grab my personal bat and enter the on-deck circle. I would stand twirling my bat and adjusting my helmet, looking into the batter's box, simply waiting for my name to be called.

My mentality—and swagger—started to grow once I knew that I could hit the ball and make a difference in the ball game. At times fellow teammates who batted before me would use the tee, and I can remember grinning with pride as the tee was pulled to the side during my approach to the plate. Clasping my hands to the bat and positioning my feet next to the plate, I would anxiously await the first pitch. Our league used bright yellow pitted baseballs, but the time of day affected my ability to see the ball. Daytime games made it tougher for me to visually pick up the ball when it exited the machine. In my mind, the nighttime was the right time because I could see the ball through at least 80 percent of its trajectory through the air. Pausing, I would wait and listen for the sound of the ball being released onto the spinning wheel of the machine. There were always two separate sounds: one when the ball touched the wheel and one when the ball exited the machine. Completely dependent on my hearing, I could accurately time the arrival of the ball to the plate. This sense became so keen that there were times when I chose not to swing simply because I did not like the sound. I loved listening and matching up my timing with my swing to make solid contact with the baseball. I would consistently launch the ball into the outfield and was thinking immediately about extra bases. In fact, I discovered that it was highly possible to hit home runs in the park on a regular basis. By hitting a ball deep into the outfield or having it roll to the wall, I could add one or more runs to the board. My tee-ball coach was overwhelmed and excited by the production at the plate; he would exuberantly display his enthusiasm with each ding of the bat. I had transitioned from the kid who only found enjoyment in the free post-game Mountain Dew to a confident player on the field. What had originated as anger toward the game became an acquired appetite and fulfillment.

When I approached the age that my play in the league was supposed to end, the league made an exception and extended my years of play by one additional season. The doctors did not want me to progress to the next level of baseball. Facing a live pitcher would be risky and place me further outside of a controlled environment. I had won a team championship, a sportsmanship of the year award, and most importantly, confidence in my ability to produce. Approaching the realization that it would end was extremely heartbreaking.

In the moment, I didn't realize how much I truly gained through the experience of playing baseball. Baseball created a foundation for the powerful life lesson of listening. Pressed outside of my comfort zone, I had to learn to adapt. My circumstances were not going to change; my vision was not suddenly going to get better. Listening not only allowed me to hit the baseball but also led to a multitude of life-enriching and life-altering moments. I place listening in my top three greatest gifts. Unbelievably, I've been accused of listening too much and recalling with too much detail. The world that I know and experience always revolves around listening. Little did I know that listening would lead to my greatest victory. Thankfully, I found victory on the baseball field, but my ultimate victory over darkness was achieved by listening.

Listening is applicable for all areas of your journey. Much of my learning is directly connected to the ability to listen; however, I don't think I could label listening as a gift if I did not use it daily. And I purposely view listening as a gift; otherwise, it can be listed as a strength. A strength is something that you are known for or something that fits you well. A gift, on the other hand, is meant to be given to others. Strength adds to your life, but a gift adds to others' lives. Through listening, I have demonstrated love, compassion, and investment in others. Listening is a dynamic part of who I am and who I want to continue to be in the future. Opening my ears and purposely making mental notes has opened countless doors for me to be an instrument and blessing for other people. Through listening, I made contact with the baseball, and through listening, I have made contact with people's hearts.

Considering your own walk of life, what lessons were meant for you outside of your comfort zone? Setting aside complaining and being stressed about a season of life, what is a life lesson that came through that season? I say with conviction that it is possible you missed a crucial life lesson because you were blinded by discontentment. Do not miss the blessing and do not miss the gift that is found outside of your comfort zone!

Chapter 11

COMPELLED TO DARKNESS

A s I grew up, I increasingly became aware of my visual impairment and the distinct differences between my life and the lives of those around me. I always understood something was different about my eyes, but it was not until third grade of elementary school that it became real. After being introduced to group settings, I could not ignore the obvious fact that I was different than all the other kids. After such animosity toward my mom for signing me up for tee-ball unfolded into one of the best experiences I could have at that age, my love for baseball grew and my ability to perform on the field grew as well. Envisioning starting school without playing tee-ball because

I had aged out would have made the classroom a greater shock for me. The coaches in the local league awarded me an additional year of tee-ball since I could not play at the next level, but I was still devastated that my playing time had to end. I felt like I was losing my only ability and my only source of excitement. Through remarkable investments from the coach, I had gained confidence in the batter's box and a greater ability to field the ball. To have all those things cut short simply did not seem fair. Combining my loss of base-ball and challenges in the classroom, I began to spiral into darkness—a spiral of no's, a spiral of dead ends, and a spiral of physical and mental pain.

Frankly, I began to despise the journey that was set before me. I absolutely hated that I had a visual impairment and agonized over the mounting circumstances. No one could guarantee that I would be able to keep even a portion of my vision, and my care team was having conversations about my future prognosis and optional treatments. Such cases as mine often involve a complete loss of vision, a disease in the left eye that would cause the entire eye to shrivel up like a dried-out raisin, or the closing of the Molteno tubes. As an adult, honesty is something you can appreciate even when it hurts, but as a young boy, you want to be told that everything is going to be all right.

Now, I commend Dr. Ellis and my mom for not camou-flaging the truth at hand. They jointly set an expectation that my life was indeed going to be different and the process was going to be daunting. I couldn't help but think that I was the only one sitting in the examination chair, trapped in this horrible nightmare with nowhere to go. How could life be so cruel and unrelenting?

As the years progressed, my brother, Chad, was in the examination chair right beside me. It helped knowing that my brother was there with me and going through some of the same steps. Chad knew the sensation of having your pressures checked, the blinding light for several minutes to see the optic nerve, and the surgery for placement of the Molteno tubes. But it also brought a fork in the road for our journey. Chad's appointments and prognosis seem to be trending up, and they knew the effects of his glaucoma would not be as severe as mine. Chad's diagnosis came at age three; mine came a few days after birth. His pressures were more stable, his vision was stronger, and his operations were fewer.

It was as if I had been selected for and appointed to the darkness—a never-ending staircase I was destined to climb alone. In fact, in my childhood home, there were two staircases split by the landing for the garage and front door. I would often go downstairs to play or follow my mom as she was running loads of laundry. One day I stopped at the lower staircase and sat down by myself. Knowing my mom was outside running the lawn mower, I began to weep in silence. The day was not marked by misfortune or any type of physical pain; it was more of a wave of emotional distress that overtook my mind and heart. Turning sideways, I laid my head down on an upper step and continued to cry. Through my tears, I could see detail in the carpet fabric that I had not seen before. For me, carpet did not usually have an underlying design. I would only see one color or the prominent lines that created the most contrast to the base. This imagery specifically replicated my exact thoughts and feelings that day. My entire life was seeing only one thing while missing all the details due to my impaired vision. My clenched fist turned into a mallet, pounding the step out of anger. Reaching a point of no care, no value, and no hope, I needed an end to the despair.

Holding a pocketknife I had received from my cub scout group, I opened the main blade. Placing the blade on its side against my forearm, I began to run it up and down slowly. Then, standing the blade on its edge, I placed it along my wrist. Noticing the sharpness, I began to lightly apply pressure toward the back of the blade. Certain of my actions but clouded in my mind, I continued to run the blade along my wrist and forearm.

Out of the quiet came a sharp voice, "Kurt what are you doing?"

Mom had entered without my knowing and saw the knife in my hand. I could not provide an adequate answer other than I was just playing. Mom insisted that a knife was something we did not play with and was a tool used only during special times.

Emotional pain pulsated through my mind; therefore, subconsciously I thought it could be possible that physical pain could ease the emotional pain. Thankfully, I never inflicted self-harm, but that is where my mind was.

Along with my mental anguish, sickness seemed to be paired with the sound of my alarm. Awakening to nausea and an upset stomach was all too familiar. Like any child at that age, I experienced my share of acute illnesses such as ear infections and sinus infections, but I distinctly recall the awful feeling that persisted and only grew in intensity as pick-up time for the school bus drew near. I would tell my mom every morning that I did not feel well, and I would go through the morning feeling sick with uneasiness in my stomach. Begrudging the start of each day I would tremble that I had to make a return to school. I now know that I was struggling with stress and anxiety during those morning episodes, which fully explains the consistent answer my mom would give: "Go to school, and if you are still sick later in the day, go to the nurse's office." It is safe to say that if I had missed every day when I felt sick, I would still be making up days of school well into my thirties.

On the subject of making up days, I am still surprised I did not miss a few days of school for an outburst of rage on the school bus one day. With assigned seats, I sat next to the same boy going to school and coming home every day. This boy enjoyed taunting me and giving me a tough time about my thick glasses. Overall, I was not bullied on a regular basis by any other member of the class. He loved to call me "four eyes" and always made it a point to test my vision.

One day we were on the bus behind the school waiting for the teachers to unlock the door and I was undergoing another taunting from my seat partner. With my hunched-over position of trying to mind my own business, my seat partner decided it would be beneficial to lean in front of my face while calling me "four eyes."

At my wit's end, I used my hands to push his head away. Apparently, he was not expecting that as his head jolted backward and hit the brace in between the windows of the bus.

I was unfazed by his head hitting the brace, feeling relieved that he might finally leave me alone. Grabbing the back of his head, he said that I had broken his head open with the hit. I told him that he should have left me alone and I did not believe him when he claimed that he was hurt. Pulling his palm away from his head, he showed me a reddish residue splattered on his palm. Still not fully convinced that I had broken his head open, I asked him to turn around so that I could look. When he turned, sure enough there was a red bubble about the size of a nickel on the back of his head.

I was completely stunned. It was my very first hit and I really caused an injury and brought blood to the surface.

Fearing that I was in for major repercussions, I told him that he needed to see the bus driver. Sliding my legs into the aisle, I allowed him to get out of the seat and approach the bus driver. At that moment, my heart rate intensified, and I began worrying about what was to come. I thought for sure the bus driver would lay a welt on my backside. I could hear the driver making a call on the radio to the nurse's station and asking the principal to report to bus number sixteen. Next, thankfully without the assistance of the internal speaker system, he asked me to come to the front seat.

Slowly I rose and took the dreaded steps toward the front seat. When I got there, the driver told me to sit down and wait for the principal to arrive. Trying to hold my breath and not make a sound, I would have given anything to escape out of the double doors of the bus. The nurse and the principal of the elementary school arrived at the bus together. A brief synopsis was provided by the driver, and my classmate was escorted by the nurse while I was asked to step off the bus with the principal. Fingers wrapped around the straps of my backpack, I walked with the principal, answering her questions about what had transpired. Answering truthfully in broken bits, I explained my side of the story. When we entered her office, I fully anticipated the paddle hanging next to the bookshelf to be dusted off on my rear end. Instead, I sat down across from her and listened to her instruction and advice on the situation.

While I may not have been paddled, I did have to come clean to my mom and low-vision aid about the events of the morning. I was also asked to apologize to the classmate I hurt. Feeling remorse and disappointment, I offered my apology. I guess the principal deemed my apology to be cordial and allowed me to resume my day in the classroom.

What they did not know was that fighting had not only taken place between a classmate and me but also within myself as an internal war raged week by week. Disconnected from what appeared to be a normal life, I couldn't find security at home. Mom and I had our disagreements and scuffles, but deep down I knew that she loved me tremendously. She would always be available to talk with me and hear what I had to say, but that same security, camaraderie, and love were absent when it came to my father. Sadly, a lot of my early memories of my father are of him not being present. Even when he was present, it did not involve me. Fathers are supposed to be role models for their sons and serve as a friend.

Chapter 12

DIVISION

The days I had to miss school were designed to be the best days, even if I was missing school for a doctor's appointment. Typically, that meant my brother and I did not have to eat the school lunch; however, there were some days we missed school that were simply not enjoyable. They felt like days of missing school for sickness or the death of a loved one.

Those not-so-fun days would start with dressing like we were going to a funeral, but the destination would be the courthouse in the next county. I remember telling classmates that I would be gone the next day but not wanting to provide a reason for my absence. Diligently working to keep a barrier between my private and public life, I wanted to avoid the embarrassment of what was going on behind the scenes.

Sharing the back seat, my brother and I would sit for the one-hour ride to the courthouse. I clearly remember one time my brother held up his wristwatch, a gift I had given him earlier, pointed, and said, "It's time."

Once again, it was time to face our dad in the courtroom.

Parking spaces lined the perimeter of the courthouse lawn, cars staggered on each street. Slipping into the shadows along the west side of the courthouse, my gut would start to turn, and my heart rate would elevate. Passing through the west entrance, you were greeted by a long corridor that ran all the way to the east entrance. Gingerly climbing a set of old wooden stairs, we advanced to the second level. Sounds would ping off the walls, and the echoes were louder than any gymnasium in the state of Indiana. At the top step was the checkered flooring that lined the upper hallway. The whole time, all I could think about was that I wished we had crossed the finish line of the race against all these attacks from my dad.

Although we waited at opposite ends of the hallway, I could still hear and see my dad at the other end. It completely blew my mind that he wanted to smile and wave and try to be cheery toward me and my brother since he was stabbing us in the back. He was putting us in a repeated state of anguish for his own selfish gain.

Voices of discontent rolled through my mind and touched my eardrums as I listened to the lawyers going back and forth between the judge's chamber and clients. In a previous court meeting, I had conveyed to the judge that I no longer wanted any part of my visitation rights. My brother, on the other hand, remained handcuffed to the visitation assignments.

My decision and actions only added lighter fluid to the raging flames in my dad's heart. Determined to invoke as much pain as possible financially and emotionally, he freely made motions for complaints and filed suits against my mother. Finances were at the center of every entanglement. Health coverage was a fight, child support was a fight, and college expenses were shifted entirely to me and my mom. Excelling at severing the line of love, my dad crafted a recipe for anger in my heart. Battling low vision took a back seat to a bigger opponent in my own father. How could he be so numb and unforgiving in his pursuit to put us in the line of fire?

There was one day when my thoughts were spiraling out of control. The anger began to bubble in intensity, and my fists clenched to the point of shaking. Thoughts quickly transitioned to calloused confrontation, removing the weight of any spoken word. Positioned on top of my dad's toes outside of the courtroom, I proceeded to erupt in outrage: "How could you do this to us? Don't you see how much hurt you are causing? You've done nothing but let Satan overtake your thoughts and actions."

Unfazed by my words, he stood there and batted his eyes. In that moment, I felt myself wanting to bring physical harm to him.

Months removed, horror cycled through my brain when I thought about inflicting physical pain. By far, some of my most unhealthy thoughts culminated around my dad. I was mentally at the edge of a cliff, convinced the fall would be worth the relief. Division was not only physical but also psychological. I could not identify with myself, my emotions, or my character. Inhibiting my presence was the darkness, sadness, and humiliation of being connected to this person they called my father.

Stamping out the reckless desires, I instead drew a line between our paths, creating a separation of our lives. I longed for freedom and a brighter day that sprung forth new air. Independently I had shut down and clipped my body armor on, protecting my life. Seeking new ground and new direction, I fled, for I knew what was ahead had to be better than that.

Including my dad in my personal life had become a weight that I no longer wished to carry. The weight was not only measured in pressure but also in times of emptiness.

During my freshman year of high school, I was on the football team as a student manager. On Friday nights I would stay after school while the varsity team competed. On the nights we had a home game, we would go to a local restaurant for a pregame meal. Kickoffs always occurred at 7:30 p.m., and typically my duties would finish around 10 or 10:30 p.m. After one game, as I climbed the stairs behind the fieldhouse, I began to look for my dad in the parking lot as it was his visitation weekend. With limited vision and inhibitors, night vision is a major struggle. I knew that my dad would pull into a parking spot rather than pull up to the curb. During this time, he drove a dark blue car, which did not stand out at night. Halos and crystal balls of light would form around other car lights, which made it hard for my eyes to focus and scan for the appropriate car. On this night, I could not find where he was parked; therefore, I walked down the sidewalk slowly trying to scan each car. After an extended period of not being able to find him, I tried to call him. There was no answer on the other end, so I left a voicemail. I proceeded to call our home phone, but there was no answer there either.

I had no clue where my dad was, and I could not find him or get him to answer his phone. After another extended period, I headed back down the stairs to knock on the locked double doors outside of the locker room, hoping someone would hear me. Able to grab the attention of one of the janitors, I walked back to the coach's office. Surprised to still see me in the complex, I told him I couldn't find my ride. He invited me to sit on the couch and continue to call.

Finally, my mom called me back; she had just finished working at a local business she would provide cleaning services for late on Friday nights. I said, "Mom, Dad isn't in the parking lot, and I waited for a long time."

After assuring me she was on her way to pick me up, she tried to call my dad since my brother was with him already. Finally answering the phone, she learned my dad had gone home, which was thirty minutes away, because he was cold and fell asleep. Never did he come down to the fence to tell me nor did he send me a text message. With temperatures already rising in our relationship, this was a continuation of him not showing up on my behalf.

This event may seem like a small misunderstanding, but for me it was a turning point. I did not want to be let down anymore. Refusing to have my dad return to New Castle to pick me up, as it was late and I had a junior varsity game in the morning, I went home with my mom. The inches in my dad and I's relationship became feet, and feet became yards.

With my interest and participation in sports, the word "accountability" was brought up on a regular basis. Athletics on the team taught me life lessons that I would need to thrive individually and professionally. As a student manager, I was solely responsible for carrying out my duties regularly, on time, and at the highest level of efficiency. Working with a set schedule lined with personal duties for the sake of the team also instilled an elevated level of accountability. Matching my responsibilities with my effort, attitude, and attention meant there was an expectation that I was going to be present to meet each need. Me, myself, and I would be held accountable for all activities as a student manager, including moments of oversight or wrong decision.

Maturing in my own cognitive development, I struggled with listening to my father dismiss accountability. His verbiage and mannerisms were nothing but a sales pitch pressuring me to understand his misery.

I understand that hurt, disappointment, and embarrassment always take place in a separation, but transferring that pressure to your kids causes deep wounds. In the earliest days of visitation, I remember my dad being furious with my mom and trying to drag her into his apartment saying, "I want you to see what you have done to me." Living through misplaced motives and the untouched realm of accountability, I lost the desire to be connected to my dad in a normal father–son relationship.

In complete transparency, I was disgusted by the actions of my father and wanted to build my own life and my own accountability. Starting my junior year of high school, I pulled away and expressed my desire that he maintain his distance.

That distance was achieved, but there was no denying that hurt remained. Occasions like senior night and graduation necessitated uncomfortable explanations for why my father was not invited. There were a select few who would understand, but many couldn't understand my choice, and a few always wished they had the decision to invite their dads. Regardless of their reaction, all these encounters revisited a broken and dysfunctional family history that I wanted to disassociate with.

Embarrassment about my relationship—or lack thereof— with my father outweighed the self-consciousness from my visual impairment. Medically speaking, it was as if I had wounds across my body. I could work to cover the wounds and they did not hurt as much if contact was not made. Yet, healing was not taking place because unwelcome reminders would come forward, telling me I was still hurting, I was vulnerable, and a treatment had not been applied. How could there be a treatment for something that I did not create in the first place? I didn't know how to fix a relationship I separated myself from, desiring peace and accountability, and it was impossible for me to pretend to have a normal father–son interaction.

Over a decade has passed since I made the personal decision to disconnect from my dad's presence. The initial decision was not difficult, but my conduct and decisions in the years following the separation proved to be difficult.

There was a lot of focus on forgiveness based on the forgiveness that Christ provided all of us. Trying to explain my position, my hurt, my worries, and my weariness, I sought Godly advice. Dedicating time to my pastor, respected elders, and close friends, I would ask for clear direction. Repeatedly I would become entangled in the dynamic of forgiveness and forgetting. Could I have truly forgiven my dad without being in communication with him? Was it okay to continue to say "wait" to my earthly father but "yes" to my heavenly Father? Where is the line between protection and peace?

I want to say that I have the answer, that I have some sort of revelation for you, but that simply is not true. There is still minimal contact between me and my dad by personal choice today; however, what I do have today is a restored peace because of the treatment of forgiveness.

The measure of my forgiveness was discovered in the wounds. Bandages could cover my wounds, but that did not mean they were healed. Many folks today live life with wounds that have never been treated. One of my biggest points of emphasis is that you can only control your response. How do I know that people live with open wounds? I hear their response and I don't need to see to know treatment has not been applied. In the same ways as them, I used to lash out and live in pain as I was dealing with my wounds. Forgiveness was only made clear to me when I looked at Jesus Christ. Following His death upon the cross and His resurrection, the disciples could see the scars on Jesus as noted in Luke chapter twenty-four. Forgiveness was in place, but the scars remained.

Through Christ's forgiveness, we are brought to new life, but it does not mean the puncture points disappear. Personally, I no longer wanted to hang onto the wounds. I opened my heart and body to healing. I want to open my testimony and life, not to claim warrior status but to claim a wonderful God who delivers abundantly. Something that was a problem became a praise; it was a pillar, but now it is a path. While I still seek to understand how to move forward relationally, I do know a change has occurred and the wounds are healed.

It is now a praise that division became revision in my journey. Fellow men willingly stepped into my life and became a father figure for me. Receiving wisdom, truth, and unparalleled support, I have stood at the floodgates of blessings. Where I was once left behind, I am now elevated to a genuine love that can never be matched nor replaced. God demonstrated His love for me through fellow men who met needs far greater than my comprehension. My soul rejoices in the deep and rich connections that have been established.

Through my life experience and upbringing, I am extremely sensitive to the reality of divorce and shattered homes. I feel a responsibility, as well as a sense of purpose, to invest as I have been invested in. Desiring to sow in love, I am convicted to be used by God to help others in crisis situations. Birthed out of division is a refreshed mind, spirit, and compassion for others who find themselves in a similar position. Embrace the scars and embrace that things are going to look much different than you imagined. Just because you are standing at a different location than you planned does not mean you are in the wrong place. God uses the limitations for his glory, and he uses the division for revision.

Chapter 13

WHERE ARE THE LINES?

I dentifying lines is something that has been visually challenging for me. Most people assume that small print is hard to read, but what people don't know is that it can be just as hard or even harder to see lightly colored lines. One example is the fancy checks that have a picture in the background and the lines for writing out the check are very faint. I cannot tell you how many times I needed a magnifying glass to locate the lines on a check or on a receipt at a restaurant. In fact, when I need to sign a receipt, I know the line is somewhere about three-fourths of the way down the receipt. Let's just say I am guilty of a large signature to make sure that I cover the appropriate line. However, this doesn't help when I need to leave a tip and identifying the appropriate line is necessary. When I was in school, they made accommodations for me to ensure that I could see the lines. They ordered special memo paper with bold, dark lines and I was allowed to use ink pens for my assignments. Without the darkened lines, it was hard for me to leave an appropriate mark; my writing would be scrambled and seemed to have little direction.

In another example, fishing is an activity I have grown to love, but like printed lines, fishing lines are difficult to see. Bright light is always necessary for restringing a pole or tying on a new hook. While fishing, I always keep my thumb and first finger on the line and depend on touch rather than sight.

After my brother got his driver's license, I was so excited because that meant I had some wheels. I would always try to convince my brother and my mom that we needed to go somewhere. One summer morning my brother and I got up early to head to Westwood Lake to do some fishing after talking about it the night before. Usually, we would take the boat to reach our favorite part of the lake, known to us as the crappie tree. The crappie tree was located in a back cove of the lake, and we thought it wouldn't be too difficult to walk to if we cut through the woods. Grabbing our fishing gear from the back of the pickup truck, we headed out.

After about thirty minutes, we finally got as close as we could to the crappie tree fishing location. Along the bank there was a good amount of tree coverage and there were limbs that obstructed a clear hole to fish through. Do you think this would stop two young boys from fishing though? We worked to slide down a slippery bank to get closer to the water's edge.

Excited to get our lines in the water, we began to have hope for that first nibble. Typically, I was the first one to catch my line on a tree or have a knot at the end of my pole. However, on this fishing adventure, my brother was the first one to catch his line above his head in a tree. Ordinarily this wasn't a problem since my brother could see the line to get it out or string a new line, but we quickly discovered that my brother had forgotten his tackle box in the truck and since we were a thirty-minute walk away, we didn't want to break the line.

Looking for ways to improvise, I saw a dead tree that could be pushed over. Of course, I needed something to bend the limb down above my brother's head since neither of us was tall enough to grab the limb that the line was wrapped around. Once we were able to maneuver the limb down far enough, we disconnected the line that was caught. Then came the bright idea of adding another log to the lake. I tossed it in before remembering that I might scare the fish away. Caught up in being funny, the adventure turned from fishing to creating mischief. At that point, we decided to abandon our location and move back up to the bank to a much clearer area that had a rocky edge that was easy for bank fishing. At the end of my pole was a bobber about the size of a tennis ball. I wanted to make sure that I could see the bobber move upon a bite.

Reaching the clear area, my brother and I spread out to cast in opposite directions. I was located on the eastern side of the mound while my brother was located on the western side of the mound. We could easily converse and hear each other's voices, but we could not see each other fishing. The glare on the lake was intensifying as the sun was coming up in the morning; therefore, I knew that I would have to depend upon feel for the line even though I had a giant bobber. I knew without a doubt that the trophy fish was in the middle of the lake, and I absolutely had to place my bobber and hook in that location. Raring back to send a ginormous cast, I flung my line forward toward the middle portion of the lake. Hearing the whisking sound, I was proud of a well-placed cast until I heard a pop and clink. Suddenly my fishing line was nowhere to be found. I heard the plunge from the large bobber, so I knew my line was out there somewhere. Running my right hand and fingers along the pole I quickly understood there was no line attached to my reel. I called my brother's name three or four times. My brother came around the corner and asked, "What is the matter?"

I told him, "I don't know what happened, but I can't find my line."

With a puzzled and chuckling response, my brother said, "Your bobber is almost halfway across the lake!"

The inside part of the reel must have clipped my line as I flung the heavy bobber and sinker forward. This travesty meant that my fishing experience was done for the day since we did not have the tackle box with us. We ended our fishing prematurely and decided that it was time to head out. Never fear—we did get a big bite as we went through the McDonald's drive-through for breakfast. We always laugh about this fishing occasion when we accomplished absolutely nothing.

As I got older, I would ask myself, "Where are the lines in my life?" Exactly like that morning on the lake, I was continually casting my line and placing my fingers on it looking for a pull. Blinded by the glare and my blurred vision, I was just searching for something to hang on to. How was I supposed to catch something when the line was not present? Is this life just a series of casts without anything to show for it? No one had to tell me that life was picking up pace and soon a time would come when decisions would need to be made. I was fully aware of the daunting future that lay before me. Was progression possible if my life was completely out of line? I was experiencing complete darkness and feared what I could not see. No matter how much I threw my line, nothing came my way. The line was cut, and the abundance of life was no longer attainable.

If I could have only known the future when I was entrenched in those lost feelings, I would have seen that eventually things would make complete sense. I would know how I would take hold of the greatest catch that would indeed completely change my trajectory.

Requiring bright light to identify the lines would come full circle in understanding where my life needed to be. Just as lines are present on the highway to ensure traffic moves in order, so are lines necessary in a person's life. There must be boundaries to keep a person on the pavement and help them avoid destruction. The road map to this life is a lot closer than you may expect. The saying that "difficult roads can lead to the best places" is certainly true; the past can be rather bumpy, but it can also be worth it when you know the destination that awaits at the end of the highway.

Chapter 14

LIGHT ORIGINATES FROM THE SON

Then spake Jesus again unto them, saying, I am the
light of the world: he that followeth me shall not walk in
darkness, but shall have the light of life.

–John 8:12

Church attendance or involvement was limited during my childhood. Sundays were simply another day in the week; there was no thought given to worship or setting them aside as the day of the Lord. Prayer was not something regularly exercised—not during personal time, at the dinner table, or before bed. My earliest associations with Christianity always took place at my grandparents' house on my mother's side. Going to my grandparents' house always seemed like a step back in time, but that never detracted from the excitement of knowing that I was headed to their house for an overnight stay. A descent upon Grandma and Grandpa's house meant climbing the apple trees in the orchard, shooting blackbirds off the telephone wire, driving a rebuilt lawn mower my grandpa made for us, and taking a walk down to the nearby creek to hang out under the bridge. Television was not an option, so we always created our own entertainment. I remember my grandma being more nervous about administering my eye drops than she was about shooting a gun or driving the lawn mower. I would be concerned with where Grandma's teeth went while she was concerned about getting the drops in my eyes. Bless her heart, she did a terrific job though.

Along with a wonderful job taking care of me, eating at our grandparents' house was always a winning scenario. I was introduced to a little something called snack time! I learned that you could spray cheese out of a can onto a cracker or you could pour a bowl of sugar for the sole purpose of dunking strawberries. Other times we would take a small road trip to the world's best hot fudge sundae drive-up or make a pit stop at the old-fashioned candy store. Everything about those spring break visits and summer days always seemed so sweet. But the most prominent memory is the timeframe before we would go to bed.

Every night we would gather in the living room for a time of prayer. I would always run to the rocking chair to claim my spot. While praying in a kneeling position, having the rocking chair ensured I could still move during the long prayers. At the time, I didn't fully understand the reason for prayers or my grandparents' commitment to doing so every night. I did recognize that the way of living I was accustomed to at home was clearly different than that of my grandparents. It wasn't only the absence of technology and the simplicity of living but also the choice not to use any medical intervention. As I grew older, I began to have these conversations with my grandparents. I wanted to know and feel the same emotions they did. Especially during the transition of my mom divorcing my biological dad and remarrying, I began to capitalize on the opportunity to ask questions and formulate a better understanding of not only my mom's upbringing but also my grandparents' convictions. This is when I started to develop a spiritual appetite.

After my mom remarried, we relocated to New Castle to live with my stepdad and attended church regularly. I was exposed to God's Word not only during Sunday School or church services but also through the vacation bible school program. Pondering the differences between my grandparents' teachings and the teachings at that church, I found it hard to know what was right. I knew that practically speaking, if my mom had not taken medical action, I would have never known what it was like to have vision at all. Even though what I have is limited sight and blurred vision, her fight still enabled me to keep a precious gift in this life. Setting the differences in teachings aside, I decided it was worth my time to simply enjoy the benefits of attending church activities.

My heart goes out to individuals and families who have questions about living the Christian life. What does it really mean to be a Christian? How can I have peace and security in my life? Is it true that a person can really know they have a home in heaven once life is ended?

All of these and more are particularly important conversations to have. The world today is cluttered and divided by a myriad of complexities. According to the most recent census, close to 39 percent of marriages in the United States end in divorce. In 2017, the National Survey on Drug Use and Health (NSDUH) calculated that 19.7 million Americans battled a substance use disorder. Also, according to the NSDUH, in 2019, over 25 percent of adults eighteen and older were classified as heavy or binge drinkers of alcohol. The implications of these statistics then have a financial impact on individuals and families. Sadly, it is easy to see that pain and despair lives across this land; people are continuously searching for hope. It would be fair to assume that many of the individuals affected by the statistics above have at least been to a church service once or had a family member who was involved in a local church. Meanwhile, livelihoods are caught in the darkness, being consumed by fear and selfish motives.

History, including darkness, is something every single human shares. Our stories may be developed or written differently, but we've all experienced life-changing moments and seasons that construct that history. And more often than not, we realize there is crossover and overlap between our stories. What has been broken and shattered can be restored. Darkness does not have to consume your entire life and your entire story.

In fact, your trials will become your tests that will eventually produce your testimony. We all have a past, but we also have a future. The past cannot be rewritten, but the past can write your future. Will it be written in darkness, or will it be written in light? That is the crossroads where you must make a personal decision—a decision no one else can make on your behalf, a decision that redirects your mind, heart, and spirit. This decision is not a temporary change but a new life that dwells in the brightness and vigor of a new story.

The crossroads—the need for a decision—was made known to me by the cross. The design of the cross is simple, yet it signifies the world's most powerful message. Even through blurred vision, the physical emblem of the cross can still be recognized. Absent physical vision, the open eyes of the heart discover Jesus at the center of the cross. As a set of cross hairs, the intersection of the cross puts a target on man's sin, which is at the center of man's struggles and ultimate separation from God. God sent His one and only son, Jesus, to take up the cross and place himself in front of man's sin. It is through Jesus that darkness becomes light. He suffered the agony of His own weight hanging upon the nails, He suffered the crown of thorns being pressed into His head, He suffered the lashing, and He withstood mocking and public humiliation. He became an unrecognizable human figure saturated by His own blood and hanging tissue, all to overcome the world's sin. His love never ran out, His speech against his adversaries never rang out, and His power to escape was never enacted. Jesus Christ endured until the end so that our sins would be covered in the blood by the Perfect Lamb. Christ willingly took on our sin so that we could have life. Without the cross, we would have no hope and we would shoulder the pain from our waywardness. The message of the Gospel is quite simple: God sent his Son into the world not to condemn it but to provide life. Look at the following verses.

> For God so loved the world, that he gave his only begotten Son, that whosoever believeth in him should not perish, but have everlasting life. For God sent not his Son into the world to condemn the world; but that the world through him might be saved.
> *–John 3:16-17*

After several weeks of attending church, I began to experience personal conviction. My need for a savior was evident, and my shame grew heavier by the day. My comprehension of the Bible and its teachings was next to nothing, but I could not deny the Spirit moving through me. Internally I attempted to rationalize these occurrences and find a way to escape what I know now was conviction from the Holy Spirit. Only focusing on the potential embarrassment and my lack of knowledge, I tried to overcome those days by suppressing what I knew and not sharing it with peers, but this became a daily consideration and impression that I could not escape. I reasoned with myself that I was going to wait it out and just see if this was something that persisted.

During a Sunday morning service at Temple Baptist Church in New Castle, Indiana, the preacher delivered a message that was designed for me—at least I perceived it that way.

Every word that was preached landed on my doorstep. The theme of the message was derived from Revelation 3:20. Due to my lack of vision, my hearing has become a strong suit. The verse in Revelation draws the illustration of God knocking on the door. Whoever hears his voice and answers will let God in. Beyond any doubt, I knew that God had been knocking on the door of my heart, but I had yet to answer him. I had stood inside in silence, too nervous to call back out.

Did I want to invite God in?

During the alter call, the simple question was offered: "Will you answer when God knocks at the door?"

Well, guess who came knocking that Sunday morning? With the strike of the piano keys and the rising voices during the invitation time, I felt God knocking on the door of my heart. Fingers clasped to the pew in front of me, I received three knocks—or rather, three verses of song.

Almost certain my feet would remain planted in my position, I leaned forward to whisper to my mom during the third verse. Stuttering, I whispered that I needed to go forward and I wanted to accept Christ as my Savior. She asked if I wanted her to go up with me, and I told her "no" but asked if my stepdad could go. Walking toward the front of the church, I met the pastor and told him that I wanted to trust Christ as my Savior, for I knew that He was knocking. Kneeling at the steps of the altar, the pastor presented me with a few verses from Romans and asked if I believed what was written. I said "yes," and he asked if I would like to pray to receive salvation for myself.

Tears began trickling down my face. I prayed a simple prayer acknowledging my sin and His calling at the door and my willingness to invite Him in. The abundance of joy and calm overshadowed the questions about why I was moved to tears. When I rose to my feet, the pastor patted me on the back and asked if he could make an announcement that I had prayed to trust Christ. I assume that I responded positively to his question, but I was still trying to collect myself. Members of the congregation formed a line after the service to greet me and offer hugs. Each person was elated to speak with me and share in the joy that I had made a profession of faith.

The light that I once knew from the moon and the stars as a young child pales in comparison to the light that now shines in my life from the Son.

God knows where you have been, and he knows every detail about your life. Nothing can come between the completed work on the cross and Christ's endless love for you. Will you answer the call when He knocks at the door? He is the Judge who can and will pardon all sins. Humble your hearts before Him and He will welcome you regardless of your transgressions.

The acceptable time is now. When you hear that knock, do not delay in answering. Gladly open the door and welcome Him into every corner of your life. Are you listening at this moment? Are you willing to let Him bring light into your life?

Chapter 15

NEW LIFE IN CHRIST

Therefore if any man be in Christ, he is a new creature: old things are passed away; behold, all things are become new.

–2 Corinthians 5:17

Trusting in Jesus Christ as my personal Savior gave me real vision for the very first time. My feet had been removed from the sinking sand and onto solid rock. My hands that were waving aimlessly found a friend who would grasp them and be my guide. My world was brought out of the darkness and into the magnificent light. Never have I experienced such joy and peace in my life. All I knew before was struggle and pain—complete dissatisfaction with the journey I had been given. I still remember when I knelt on the steps of the altar and personally asked Jesus Christ to save my soul.

I had no expansive knowledge of the Bible or spiritual truths. Yet, beyond any doubt, I knew that God had been pressing and convicting my heart for many weeks. I knew the decision had been clearly placed in front of me and He had been continually knocking on the door of my heart. As he knocked many times, I stood frozen, hoping he wouldn't be able to find me. Truthfully, there were even times when I would figuratively run to the back room and try to hide under the bed as he knocked. I am so thankful God continued to come back and knock on the door of my heart. God knew exactly where I was, but He patiently waited for me to respond.

Through God's Word, I realized that I had to make a personal decision to let Christ into my life. Nobody in my life could make that decision for me. Considering that tomorrow is never promised, during that Sunday morning service, I made the decision to open the door of my life to Jesus Christ.

In later chapters, I focus on the keys to higher living, which deal directly with a response; however, the most important response you can have on this side of eternity is trusting Christ as your personal Savior. Make him the light of your life at this very moment!

Why is this the most important response? Simply put, the flesh you reside in today has an expiration date, but your soul remains. Jesus came and died on the cross because he did not want a single soul to be lost and experience eternity separated from him. By the way of the cross, he provided an opportunity and a way to have freedom in your life. As soon as we acknowledge that we were born into sin and that we need a Savior to forgive us of our sins, our soul is anchored in the promise of living with Christ forevermore. We do not have to pay the penalty for our own sinful nature as that price was paid upon the cross. A new creature is born when we turn our lives over to Jesus Christ. Praise God that all things become new!

My first step of obedience was participating in baptism. Desiring to make a public profession of my faith, I was brought forth out of the waters, signaling new life in Christ. The days of being trapped in the shackles of sin were no more. I had been purchased by the blood of Christ and made a new creature through Him.

Gone were the days when I had to shoulder the punishment for my own sins. Celebrating turning from sin to God, I rejoiced with fellow believers in the baptismal service. Hope was restored for both my time on this earth and for eternity. Free from my darkness, discontent, and selfish ways, I had been rescued. This public profession was not only meant for the baptismal service but was a beginning to my days of proclaiming the goodness and promise I had been given. The phrase "sharing is caring" could not be truer. Once we are saved, there is a desire deeply rooted in our soul that causes us to care deeply for all humankind. I want to share the source of my freedom, and I want to give credit to the One Above All.

Society likes to make things complicated and convoluted, but the plan of salvation is simple. In fact, the Bible states it only takes a childlike faith. Compelled to share the Gospel and to lead people to a path of joy motivates me every day. The solution resides in every believer's heart, but it must be shared! This cannot be locked away from the population any longer. The solution is at our fingertips, touching the pages of Scripture. When the curtain of sin is lifted from the eyes, a new life begins.

Becoming a new creature in Christ meant a brand-new joy overpowering everything. On that Sunday morning, rising to my feet, I began to know real joy. Continually drawing from the well of joy, I never turned back, nor do I thirst for fulfillment. I have discovered that being rich is fully obtainable because wealth is not connected to a monetary value. One is made rich by the joy of knowing the Lord Jesus Christ as your personal Savior. When this remarkable joy is inside you, it will be evident in your attitude and interactions with those around you. The love of Christ is displayed in the ever-present joy in your being.

The words of distress might be absent, but the message is louder than ever when observing the flow of people in the world. Seemingly left to shoulder their burdens alone and trapped in a vicious cycle, their joy has been stolen by the cares of this world. The good news is, no one must be a superhero and conduct life alone. Becoming a new creature also means learning a new way of communication. We instantly have access to God through prayer, and He is our friend who hears our prayers. No one should have to walk alone on this side of eternity. Receiving the hope and joy that comes directly from knowing the Lord is invaluable.

Grateful that old things passed away, I was excited to step onto a new path. Honestly, at that moment, I felt like things were going to change. I saw it as a favor or like better days ahead; it was the hope that I longed for. Certainly, once a person has trusted Jesus Christ as Savior, they do have favor in His sight, but that does not mean that things will be smooth sailing. It doesn't mean infirmities will be removed, heartaches left behind, or moments of doubt will not occur. Rather, it means that you can put on the whole armor of God and move forward in confidence.

One of the most prominent thoughts that consumes my mind is how God uses what the world calls broken. For what Satan is claiming victory in today, God will use as an ultimate source of victory for tomorrow.

Thinking back to the disciples who followed Jesus during his days on earth, Jesus selected the ones their fellow men would not select. Old things pass away because of the love that we discover. As we faithfully trust His Word, we run ahead, knowing that God is and will do magnificent work. No tower, obstacle, or valley can hide the absolute confidence that exists in Christ.

Faith is built on forgiveness—and forgiveness alone. My mind turns to the time when Jesus was nailed to the cross. Encountering unimaginable physical pain and verbal abuse, Jesus' voice still rang out: "Forgive them for they know not what they do." Jesus not only died to forgive all sins but he also reminded us on the cross how important forgiveness is. When we evaluate ourselves and recognize our records of sin but then think about God's grace and forgiveness, how powerful and humbling that is.

Does it hit home that you do not deserve forgiveness? Is your record too blemished to receive forgiveness?

Thank goodness we know that no sin is too great in God's eyes to be forgiven. In 2 Corinthians 5:15, we see that He died for all. Without the perfect sacrifice for all of humanity, we would indeed meet judgment for our own transgressions. Forgiven first by Christ, we should also be quick to forgive those in our lives. At this very moment, I'm sure you can identify someone who has caused you great harm or even someone who you have personally invoked hurt on. Remember that Christ still wants to forgive for errors in sin.

While living with congenital glaucoma has been a significant challenge, going through the process of dealing with my dad has absolutely been the most excruciating—to know and experience a dad who did not want to invest in his first son, left the door open for physical abuse through molestation, and entered a reckless pursuit for revenge through the court system. It is a portion of life that I have tried to escape from, a series of events and years I wish had never occurred. The socially appropriate action is to bite your tongue, keep a positive face, and don't let your past bring you down. While this might be appropriate for the masses, this is not appropriate according to God's Word and example. Biting your tongue or keeping a positive face does not equal forgiveness. I have learned that my forgiveness cannot be based on another individual's actions and or decisions. Reaching a point of complete forgiveness for my dad has been a journey. I sought counsel from pastors, elders, and people I trust in my search for the right answers. Over time I discovered that the only right answer came through forgiveness. I have taken every care, every burden, and every emotion and laid them before God. Today I can say that I have fully forgiven my dad and there is no ill will in my heart. It is my hope that my dad can reach a place of forgiveness as well and not live in a past saturated with hurt and blame. Broken homes and families are far too common in today's world. How many of us know a friend or fellow family who has encountered divorce in turbulent situations? Hurt feelings are abundant in people who live with the bitterness that is a by-product of these horrible situations, and forgiveness is the key that releases the handcuffs of unrighteous actions.

Resisting a moment of forgiveness also means resisting God's provision on your behalf. God is just and forgives all unrighteousness. So, when we follow the example of Christ, we must also forgive.

Soon I discovered that forgiveness is not only for one occasion or one circumstance. In fact, forgiveness absolutely must be a part of who we are because of who we trust. This can be especially hard when asking for forgiveness from another person. While I love my job at Indiana University, there have been moments of distress. There was one instance when I became enraged and allowed this to spill over toward a fellow coworker. Considering the interactions later that night, I knew that I had to ask for forgiveness. Even though that coworker may not have taken offense to what I said or deemed it a personal attack, in my heart I knew that I needed to make it right. The very next day, I approached this individual and explained my heart and emphasized that was not the right attitude.

How many times have you experienced stress in the workplace and made a quick remark or action? Even in areas where it is customary to move forward and eliminate it from memory, doing so doesn't make it right. Through forgiveness, love, and respect for others, make sure you make it right.

Never try to camouflage yourself with the world's tactics. Know that you are a new creature in Christ and that all things have been made new. Take joy in knowing that your testimony is seen by others, and it can make a difference for eternity.

Chapter 16

BITTERNESS BREAKS THE HOME

Be ye angry, and sin not:
let not the sun go down upon your wrath
–Ephesians 4:26

During February of my fifth-grade year, we moved to New Castle, Indiana when my mom remarried and moved into a newly purchased house with my step-dad. New Castle was a little less than a thirty-minute commute from my previous home, but the change in location also meant a change in the school system. Overall, I remember being excited about joining a new school and having a fresh start. Of course, there were nerves and questions heading into a new academic environment, but the transition was made easier by my low-vision instructor and soon-to-be fifth-grader teacher. The buddy system in the classroom worked amazingly as I was paired with a boy wearing an Atlanta Braves (Chipper Jones) t-shirt. Admittedly, it would have been better if he had been wearing a Cincinnati Reds t-shirt, but I was thrilled to be seated next to a baseball fan. The transition seemed to be going well, and I was able to make new friends in my class. I truly felt like this was a fresh start for not only my family but also for me personally. Maybe this was the adjustment I so desperately needed in my young life. For the first time, I felt connected at home and at school whereas that was not the case in previous years.

Knowing the trouble that my family had faced with my dad, my stepdad wanted to make the transition as smooth as possible. In the early days, I remember spending time outside in the barn, learning how to rewire the fishing boat trailer and playing a game of horse at the basketball court in front of the garage. In fact, we even mounted a set of floodlights along the front of the garage so that we could play basketball in the evenings. I enjoyed the attention to detail and learning typical techniques for fixing or building items.

One of the coolest projects we did was building a brand-new doghouse for my dalmatian, Princess. Her previous dog-house was in poor condition, so we decided to build her a new one when we moved into our new home. But this was no ordinary doghouse; it was more aptly labeled a dog mansion. Building this new doghouse was extremely exciting because it provided a new home for my favorite pup, and it was cool to see the entire process of building something from scratch. It was so meaningful to witness the effort that went into creating this new structure for my dog. I was becoming increasingly happy with my new surroundings and way of life.

As tensions between my biological father and I grew, I wanted to remain in New Castle even during my weekend visitations. Teenage years can be excruciating even without conflict in the home, especially with a split home where visitation is granted and there is shifting responsibility. I was enjoying my surroundings and my involvement with my new school in New Castle while a sizable percentage of the time spent with my biological dad seemed to be centered upon arguments. I wanted to move forward with life, and he continually wanted to live in the past. As he continued placing blame on my mom for the divorce, I became infuriated with his lack of sympathy for me and my brother. While he was stewing about the past, he was destroying our time together. I understood that he was hurting and that he felt a lot of pressure knowing that a stepdad was in the picture, but continually dismissing my feelings frayed the already battered relationship; therefore, as I mentioned earlier, I reached a point where I did not want to interact with my dad. My dad had become a weight that was pulling me down, and I was looking for a way to escape the turmoil. I did not want to live my life rehashing the past every other weekend or during every phone conversation. I wanted to move forward and try to enjoy what was set before me.

Little did I know that what awaited in the short term would be another challenge and an outright fear. Living in my teenage years, my thoughts and understanding were developed beyond the point of my mom's previous marriage. It is difficult for me to revisit and even describe the events that took place, but they are forever etched into my memory. I would transition from receiving no value from my father to providing support for my mom in an increasingly dangerous marriage. What had initiated as a joyous new beginning for our family ended in an escape for safety during the middle of the night. I had trusted the Lord as my Savior; He was supposed to uphold his own, right? Did God's promise mean anything, or was it just meant to make people feel better about any situation?

When I was around age thirteen, outside pressures were starting to mount in our home. There was friction between my stepdad and his kids. He was upset because they were not attending church regularly or following his instructions; however, my stepdad's youngest son pleaded to move in with us while my stepdad was dealing with some legal battles from his previous marriage.

I was already at the point where I did not want to honor visitation rights with my dad, and my dad and his new wife pursued legal action against my stepdad and mom. They argued that I had to honor the visitation rights until I was sixteen. I remember speaking to the judge in his chamber and describing my feelings, specifically stating that I no longer wished to visit my dad. The judge encouraged me to continue some form of relationship with my dad, but he could not force me to go every other weekend considering how close I was to being old enough to make my own decision. He did, however, decide that my brother had to continue with the visitation rights. After that hearing, I ended weekend stays with my dad, so my brother would go on his own for the weekend stays. To this day I feel guilty for leaving my brother alone. I did make a couple attempts later to spend a weekend with my dad, but it was always awkward when those conversations took place. As we would meet to exchange clothes bags for my brother, my dad would try to talk to me through the car window and plead for me to come along. There is nothing more awkward than sitting with your mom and stepdad, watching your brother be forced to go to visitation, and then hearing words exchanged between parents. The court battle was not over because my dad was in a reckless pursuit to get back at my mom. With me not wanting to come for visitation, he was trying to find a way out of paying child support or future college expenses. This added to the pain and the burden for my mom and stepdad. Not only was the emotional pain taking its toll, but the monetary impact was growing by the week. Pretty soon my brother became aggravated as well and did not want to visit my dad. Wanting to fight for us boys, my stepdad wanted nothing more than to tell my dad off and put him in his place.

Anger and bitterness were quickly becoming a mainstay in my stepdad's life. Facing legal battles from both his previous marriage and current marriage made life particularly difficult. That anger and bitterness were not only demonstrated at the courthouse or during times of transfers but also every evening in our home. At the time, my mom owned her own small cleaning business around the New Castle area. Suffering from chronic shoulder pain, she was weighing the decision of going back to school. Having only obtained a GED, she had never pursued a college education. After weighing the decision, she deemed it best to sacrifice for the family in hopes of obtaining future financial security with a better job that would have fewer physical demands. On board with this decision, my stepdad said that he would be there to support her and even help with needs around the house. Continuing to work and now going to school, my mom had her hands full. I could see the stress growing and frustration was becoming a regular occurrence. In addition, I could notice my stepdad's jealousy of my mom developing. People would ask about my mom's progress and success, and he would slump into a low self-esteem pity party. Increasingly, hot-button issues were created on a weekly basis—doing laundry, preparing a work lunch, or taking out the trash would be triggers for arguments. Both my mom and stepdad's demeanors were evolving into a more negative response every day.

In any situation, faults can be identified for both parties in a marriage. As an onlooker to the entire situation, I witnessed the most transformation with my stepdad. There would be periods of time I spent with my mom when there would seem to be no issue or arguments. Whether it was helping around the house or assisting with gardening, my mom and I always enjoyed the time spent together. Unfortunately, a common theme was developing in our conversations over the years about my stepdad's anger and bitterness. We would get extremely uncomfortable when he arrived home from work each evening. As soon as we heard the popping of gravel on our eighth-of-a-mile-long driveway, we would hold our breath. Nobody had to say a word; we could make a quick judgment of his attitude by the way he opened the door or placed his lunch box on the kitchen island.

It was very simple; there were two options for how the night would go. Option one was guns blazing from the minute he walked in. Option two was everyone was walking on eggshells until he blew up about something during the evening. It only got worse over time until it did not matter what we said or what we tried to do for him, the result was always a heated exchange.

In the beginning, the exchanges were primarily between my mom and stepdad, and my brother and I would take it in. When the exchanges took a more pointed turn toward me and my brother, we became calloused by these wars of words. We were never surprised to be facing another argument and would actively fire back comments to my stepdad. The dinner table had become an all-out battlefield over issues ranging from not chewing our food properly to me and my brother sharing in a laugh. It seemed everything provoked anger from my stepdad's end of the table. The hardest parts to swallow were the personal attacks that started to come on a regular basis, comments directed toward me such as: "You will be worthless just like your dad," "We will never be able to get you out of this house," or "Basketball isn't a job; you are freaking lazy." Toward my brother's side of the table flew comments like, "What's your problem big boy?" or "You think you are tough." Throwing a fit is one thing, but making personal attacks escalated the dialog across the table. Losing care and respect, I would gladly throw personal attacks right back in his face. Mimicking my strong language, it did not take long for my brother to do the same. Mom would not be pleased with either of our actions, nor for that matter, my stepdad instigating the scuffle.

Contention surpassed the dinner table and infiltrated every aspect of our lives. To be frank, we were living two different lives. At times we would face hell at home because of my stepdad's anger, but at church, school, and other places people had no reason to guess we were living in an unsettled home. Like turning a key in the ignition, my stepdad's tone could change in an instant. Sometimes we would get into our van after a church service, and before we had even left the parking lot a dispute would take place. I desperately wanted my stepdad to show his true colors at church. I was exhausted from living a lie and watching him sing behind the pulpit while knowing what was going on at the house.

Verbal attacks can leave scars that last a lifetime. No one should be subjected to a litany of verbal attacks. We are called to admonish and uplift each other, not unleash verbal attacks to demonstrate our power or correctness.

At the boiling point of our home life, there were two distinct events that led to physical harm for me and my brother. One Saturday we were helping install a dog kennel behind the barn. It was just us three working as my mom was in the house attending to other duties. Working around the entry point of the kennel, we were trying to set posts for the fencing. I was standing behind my stepdad, and he became overly angry with my brother who was working directly to his right. With a hammer in his hand, my stepdad proceeded to strike my brother on top of the head. I was completely startled by the sight and unnerved that my brother had been hit with a hammer. To be fully transparent, it was not a working blow, but it was still hard enough to hurt him. I was so mad and worried that he had caused harm in this rash and ignorant decision to hit my brother.

Quickly realizing what he had done, my stepdad became apologetic and tried to make sure my brother was okay. Grabbing the top of his head with both hands, my brother stood stiff. Of course, I would not allow this to be a secret or go unnoticed. I shared what had happened with mom, but my stepdad insisted that it was an accident and that the hammer happened to slip as he was working. I knew this was a lie since I witnessed the full set of actions. But the next instance of physical abuse my mom saw firsthand.

One night as we were preparing for bed, my brother and I were brushing our teeth at the pedestal sink in our bathroom. Arguing over space, my brother and I shifted around the sink to be first to rinse our mouth out. Granted, we were aggravating each other, but it wasn't a fight or even a loud conversation. My stepdad was passing through the hallway and overheard the exchange of words. He assumed I was the one causing the issue and pointed his finger, exclaiming that I needed to cut it out.

I responded, "This is only between us and not you."

Proceeding to shove his finger into my chest, I reacted by swatting it away. My stepdad only shoved it harder into my chest as he said, "Boy, this is my house, and you are not going to tell me what to do."

I was not going to back down, and I pushed his hand away once more. Lunging forward, my stepdad pushed me backward and I fell between the sink and the toilet. On the way down, my elbow crashed into the medicine cabinet and broke the front sliding door mirror.

Caught in a moment of disbelief and complete rage, I jumped back up and attacked him. Gathering all my might, I slammed him into the door of the bathroom and said I was not going to take it. Wrapping my arms around his torso, I had one purpose: to sling him through the glass doors of the shower behind me. Unbeknownst to me, my mom had arrived and started screaming, "Stop! Stop!"

Raging with the worst kind of anger since going toe to toe with my biological dad in the courthouse, I was prepared to send the biggest message I could by causing harm. Resecuring my grasp and my footing, I pushed him back once more, planning to continue the motion toward the shower. Suddenly I stopped as I held him in one place. Shaking and honestly completely caught off guard by my actions, I paused and relinquished my plan after hearing my mom's voice.

As my mom and stepdad exited the scene, I grabbed my right elbow. During the altercation, the mirror had cut my elbow—not a severe cut, more of just a burning sensation. I don't even particularly remember the next words from my mom. I just wanted to hide in my room downstairs alone. Laying on my side in the dark, I remember profusely shedding tears. I was devastated by the altercation. How could we move forward and not continuously think about that night?

It was like the gloves had been pulled off, and there was no going back.

Eventually my mom came into my bedroom and asked if I could come upstairs to the living room, although it was more of an instruction than a question. I was expected to head upstairs. When I entered the dimly lit living room, my mom told me to sit in the rocker on one end of the living room so that she would be in between me and my stepdad on the couch. Still upset by the situation, my mom wanted each of us to apologize and talk through what happened. I remember words being shared on both ends and feeling slightly better but also doubting that this conversation would change anything in our home.

Time became my friend when I moved to Vincennes University for my first year of college. Leaving home for the first time was an eye-opening experience—one that was hard for the first few weeks. But what wasn't hard was leaving the disputes and uneasy lifestyle with my stepdad behind.

Through phone calls with my mom, I knew that life at home had not changed. Both my mom and my brother were still facing the exact scenarios I had been experiencing in the years leading up to college. Feeling helpless, I just tried to encourage them over the phone. The only thing I really could do was be an open ear to listen. When I came home for spring break, I had a conversation over meal prep with my mom about the escalating anger issues with my stepdad and told her, "You do realize that you're headed for another divorce?"

Mom responded, "Why do you say that? Kurt, I don't want another divorce."

I didn't see things improving; I only saw a downward trend for my mom's health and mental wellbeing. Our conversations about my stepdad's episodes of anger continued through my time at Vincennes and into my years at Indiana University. To my knowledge there was never physical abuse aimed at my mother; however, there was a disturbing trend with verbal abuse and actions that would precede an evening of arguing. My mom told me about a handgun that my stepdad kept under the bed on his side and how when she would make the bed in the morning, she would discover that the gun was moved or slightly pulled out to the edge of the bed where it was visible on the floor. She was concerned about what was going through his mind during the night. My mom would either move the gun back into its place or kick it farther underneath the bed. I was slightly concerned about these reports, but I tried to find reasons why the gun might have been moved.

As time went on, my mom started calling more frequently—and so did my stepdad. One needed support and the other was trying to make sure he knew what was going on and what was being said. Flustered, I wondered why adults could not figure this out on their own. I was majoring in sports management, not marriage counseling or therapy.

On August 11, 2012, at 12:31 a.m., my cell phone gave a familiar ring that signaled a call coming through. Looking down at the arm rest of my recliner, I noticed that the caller ID said, "Mom." I had a self-worried pause and sudden lump in my throat knowing that this could not be a welcomed phone call. While I was fully awake and had not gone to bed yet, I was seconds away from entering a full-fledged nightmare.

With every worst thought running across my mind, I slid my finger across the screen to accept the call. Answering, "Hello Mom," my ear picked up her frantic and shaken voice, "Kurt, I just left the house, come on come, oh please Lord."

Trying to help her organize her thoughts and get clarity on the desperate situation at hand, I said, "Mom what is going on? You need to explain what is happening!"

In just a few moments, I learned that my mom was in her car headed down the driveway and insisting that my brother hurry up in his truck just a few car lengths ahead of her. Earlier that evening, my stepdad had another episode where he blew up and became extremely mad at my mom and brother. Mom went on to explain that he was so angered that she was scared for her personal safety and for the safety of my brother. The level of contention was so high that my mom flipped a switch mentally to go into self-protection mode.

Prior to going to bed, my mom had removed the gun from underneath my stepdad's side of the bed and hid it. This did not remove the immediate threat since there were guns stored in other rooms of the house; however, it removed the one closest to her during the night. It so happened that my stepdad discovered that the gun was missing even before laying down for the night. On his hands and knees clamoring to locate the missing gun, he was searching every square inch of the floor and surrounding space. Mom witnessed him running his hands along and inside of the bed and along the baseboard trying to locate the gun that she had removed. When she stayed silent about the ongoing search, my stepdad demanded she let him know where the gun was. Terrified by the look in his eyes and the tone of his voice, she was scared like she had never been scared before. He commanded, "That gun better be back under the bed by morning—or else!"

Fear pulsated through my mom's body as she lay in bed worrying about what was about to take place. The phone call was her letting me know that she had escaped with my brother after my stepdad fell asleep, constantly terrified and looking in the rearview mirror at my brother's truck, worrying that my stepdad had woken up and would soon be chasing after them in his own vehicle. Praise the Lord that my stepdad never woke up during those fleeting moments.

I told my mom that we could not let fear govern our next actions. Once she was safely on the road rounding the bend away from our house, I told her that we must get the police involved. Physical harm did not transpire that evening, but I insisted that this event had to be documented. Also, I was worried what my stepdad would do if he chased after them or located them during the night.

Finally coming to an agreement, my mom said that she would drive a good distance from the house and call the authorities to meet her in a public location. She hung up with me to call my brother ahead of her and provide instructions for what they were going to do. Obviously, I would not be getting any sleep that night. I told her to call me back as soon as she had something new to share with me.

The police told her not to go back to the house and to find someone else to stay with for at least the weekend. Mom made sure to tell me not to answer the phone when my stepdad called. Surprisingly, those calls did not start until about 5:45

a.m. that Saturday morning. Laying on my bed, my incoming call sounded as if a bomb was going to be detonated. Extremely worried, thoughts ran through my mind … Would he come to Bloomington to confront me or would he search for my mom and brother?

There was no mistake that we were at odds in the past, and he knew that my mom and I would stay in close communication. There were few secrets between us even though I was at college and starting my own life. Over the course of the weekend, we each had numerous calls, voicemails, and texts from my stepdad as he tried to determine what was going on. The fear could not be erased for any of us, and the act of leaving in the middle of the night could not be unwritten. After additional conversations with the authorities, they recommended that my mom stay away from the house and my stepdad. There was clear reason to believe that safety could be an issue if my mom and brother did make the choice to return. It was on Monday, August 13 that my mom rented a moving truck, gathered up as many items she could, and headed to Colorado to move in with her sister. My brother had an upcoming eye appointment in Indianapolis that my mom did not want him to miss. Plus, earlier in the summer we had secured tickets to the Bristol night race two weekends later. Trying to make the best out of a horrible situation, my mom had my brother come to Bloomington to live with me for a couple of weeks so that we could still honor the eye appointment, have each other for support, and attend the Bristol race together as originally planned. My mom did start having conversations with my stepdad, and he discovered that she had moved to Colorado. Insisting that he never meant to harm or scare anyone, he begged them to come back, promising that things would be different. It was almost three years before they got a divorce.

I would be remiss to discredit or overlook the number of troubles that took place when my mom was married to my stepdad. There were several extremely tough external circumstances that brought pressure and stress upon the family. I witnessed my mom trying to put her trust in God and a stepdad who became more bitter and angry every step of the way. Life can be cruel, circumstances can be nearly crippling, and fellow people can enact great harm against us. All that said, we cannot become angry and live a life consumed with bitterness. I learned that my stepdad would go to bed each night with anger on his mind and bitterness in his heart.

Now, no one is immune to having an episode of anger or having a series of bad days. The important part is knowing that you should never go to bed with anger and bitterness. Hug your loved ones and let them know that you care; do what is needed to make sure that you ask for forgiveness and reconcile differences. In Ephesians 4:26, the Bible tells us not to let the sun go down on our wrath, but it became an everyday occurrence for my stepdad to let the sun set while he was still seething with anger.

There is a whole list of reasons why the home was broken, but it all came down to one simple word. For it was not circumstances that broke the home but bitterness. Responsibility is always on our shoulders when it comes to responding to circumstances. Oftentimes we cannot dictate outside forces, but we do control our attitude and response to everything that comes our way. Please do not let bitterness break the home anymore. Make certain that the sun does not go down on your anger.

Chapter 17

WHERE IS OUR
DEPENDENCE FOUND?

I will lift up mine eyes unto the hills, from whence
cometh my help. My help cometh from the LORD,
which made heaven and earth.
—Psalms 121:1–2

Seemingly at every turn, the fall of 2012 and all of 2013 was intertwined with trials during a period in my life when I needed to be focused. Without any doubt, I knew that I had trusted Christ as my personal Savior; however, the lingering question remained … wasn't God supposed to take care of His own? If I remember correctly, we were promised a new life when we became new creatures. It did not seem like things were adding up. The complexities grew by the day, and the end of the rope was drawing near without enough left to tie a knot (although I was becoming so tired that my strength wouldn't even be able to secure a proper knot even if there were enough to tie one with).

Consequently, I recognized my life was taking up residence in the valley. I honestly was at the point where I thought my permanent address would be changed to life's darkest valley in the middle of nowhere. Suddenly my mom and brother lived over one thousand miles away, I was clueless about how things would unfold on the home front with my stepdad, I was stepping into my graduate studies, and I was trying to piece together employment opportunities. Most importantly, I was concerned about my mom and brother's safety and worried about them finding their footing in new surroundings. It did bring some comfort knowing that they were living with my aunt at the time. Having family members nearby would provide support and guidance for them.

Along with the turmoil surrounding the situation with my stepdad, during the spring of 2013, one of my dear friends who had become a father figure in my life had a stroke. Before the stroke, he recruited me at church to be an usher and serve as the assistant treasurer. I absolutely loved spending time with him and absorbing his knowledge and wisdom. His warm demeanor and sincerity are things that I continue to pursue in my own life. He would always grasp my hand and say, "You'll do great!" It did not matter what the conversation was about;

the answer was always the same. Following his stroke, I was to assume the role of head treasure at church. I was familiar with the front-end operations; however, I was not familiar with the fine print of the job. Every single piece of information was recorded by hand and placed in file folders. Not wanting to reveal my stress and overload, I focused on my dear friend's recovery and rehabilitation, hoping he could stay strong during this physical battle. I did not want him to feel bad for adding more to my plate in an already tough time.

That summer, I lost my grandpa on my mom's side due to injuries sustained in a motorcycle accident.

Unbelievable circumstances and events continued to pile up. I was in the valley, at least knee deep in mud. Having boots on simply would not have mattered during this time.

I would often express my discouragement to my roommate, exclaiming, "It's not worth it, man. I'm ready to take everything and throw it away!" Attempting to redirect my thinking, my roommate would try to provide encouragement. I appreciated his efforts, but I was at the point where it did not matter anymore, and I was ready to collapse on the spot. My exact mindset was, "Lord I have given enough, sacrificed enough, and been faithful. I am deserving of your favor much sooner, rather than later."

One night I was working late on a graduate research project, which was common for me, and I was just staring at the computer screen. Overwhelmed with the worries and burdens of the day, I began to pray in earnest. Most of the time, instead of praying, I would just get frustrated and pound my fist on the desk or spin in my office chair while grumbling.

Upon my earnest prayer, the Lord laid a powerful message upon my heart. I had been treating everything like I was the owner, taking full responsibility for every action and outcome. The Lord impressed on my heart, "You are not the owner; I am the owner of all things. I ask that you depend upon me and only me."

Thinking of Psalms 121, I could clearly understand that I had not adjusted my sight to seek the Lord's help. Indeed, I was in the valley, but I was keeping my head down thinking that I would bulldoze through, only seeing the muck and mire. Needing help, needing a breakthrough, I realized with the nudging of the Holy Spirit that I was not dependent upon him as I should be.

> *Dependence upon God requires*
> *an independent decision.*
> –Kurt Pangborn

While I developed the above saying a few years earlier, my commitment to that mindset was tested at an all-new level in the fall of 2020. Like many other industries, the sports and entertainment industries were affected by the pandemic. My job, which was centered around athletic ticket sales and conducting public tours of the facilities, was quickly put on hold. Moving from a no fall sports schedule to playing without fans meant crucial action was needed to mitigate the financial losses. In August of that year, I was notified that I would enter an indefinite furlough. Like many, a regular paycheck was vital for me as my bills are met monthly with little reserve.

While I never had a surplus in funds, I also did not worry about where money was going to come from. I had security in my employment and could count on a biweekly paycheck.

As expected, my direct deposits stopped, but unexpectedly, I battled with the unemployment office to receive income. The timing could not have been worse; the government was at a standstill, and no relief was on the way. I cut back on spending in every way I could think of and held onto every penny. A countdown formed in my head when the end was drawing near. Anguish and questions flowed as I asked, "God, I remained faithful in my workplace and tried to honor you. How can this be the result? I remain dependent upon you to work this out, but please realize I'm down to twenty-three days, twenty-two days, twenty-one days, and Lord time is running out fast!" I tried to hold strong to my faith, but feelings of doubt started to draw near. No matter how many phone calls or other attempts I made to resurrect the unemployment issue, I was placed in waiting. I could not see how God was working on my behalf, how his delay was not denial. I could only perceive how things were not working in my favor and emptiness was looming on the horizon.

But if we could see the future, we would not need faith.

Carefully constructed, God had a design in mind to take my dependence to a new level. My financial needs were met in the most unexpected, providential way. Collected in an afternoon of tears, I knew that God had heard my plea. He knew my standing and heard my heart of questioning.

I realized God could have worked in any manner, but he placed His hands on my shoulders and said, "Trust me, Kurt."

Every element of that monetary blessing pointed to a dynamic design set forth by a faithful Father in heaven.

The monetary portion took care of my collection of bills, but the faith lesson left unprecedented value in my walk with Christ. My feeble mind could not understand that God's plan was far greater than I could imagine. Bridging the gap financially was just the beginning of His blessings. I had projected an end when God presented a beginning. While I was down, he was preparing to lift me up.

I started this book with a spotlight on my physical limitation, and now I share the same limitation mindset being unveiled in my career. What I saw as a limitation was an opportunity to be promoted to a new way of life that used my gifts for His glory. I was aligned with the Perseverance Speakers Academy and placed in a position to put my heart into printed words. I got to enact my love for people, and what started as a furlough became a future. My dependence was tested and tried, but no longer will I live without using my talents and gifts for His glory. I will declare His goodness and preach that the process is worthy of consistency. Resting in His amazing grace, we depend, watch, and walk beside an awesome God.

Above all, we place our faith and trust in the completed work at the cross. The precious shedding of His blood is the atonement for not only my sins but the sins of the entire world. Overcoming death, He rose from the tomb on the third day. He is a living God who expects us to lift our eyes up toward Him for help. Make the decision to lift your eyes and set your gaze upon Christ. Rejoicing in repentance is a lifelong praise that shall never be silenced in our speech.

Furthermore, where is our rejoicing in God's provision in our lives? Like me and too many others in the world, it is quite possible you are shouldering the weight, attempting to push through demanding times without looking up and asking for help. The easy answer for why is stubbornness, yet I see pride as the biggest issue at hand. Playing mind games, we like to trick ourselves into thinking that we know best.

Who can have our best interest in mind besides ourselves? Just give me a little more time and let me devise a better path forward.

Set pride aside and find help in the One who is awaiting your cry! Trust Him for his saving grace and trust Him to be your rescue in the valley, all the while remembering who exactly we are lifting our eyes toward.

We are looking to He who is the Creator of heaven and earth. Owner of it all, He brought ease to the roaring seas, and so will He bring peace for you and me. He is waiting for us to readjust our eyes and ask for help. Our trouble is so small in God's eyes, but it is significant in His heart. Depend on Him to raise you up in your season of trouble.

We must ask ourselves a profound but simple question: where is our dependence found? Responses can be categorized into two camps.

The first is someone with their head down, shoulders slumped, and eyes looking into the mire that stretches around their feet, looking for just a small stretch of less resistance. Days waning, they continue to abide in the struggle.

The second is someone who halts their self-movement and looks up to the hills for help that comes from the Lord. Completely, with a full heart, they profess, "I am depending upon the Lord. There is no challenge and no limitation that impedes the Creator of it all. I trust you, Lord, to be my help, to be my guide, and to be my rescue. Oh, I know, there is never a request that is too extreme or too hard. I am depending upon You to move the mountain, make a way, and clean the mud from my feet. For the only thing I hold is my dependence upon You, for I see that's all I need."

Chapter 18

LINKS TO THE NAME

Wherefore God also hath highly exalted him and given
him a name which is above every name: That at the
name of Jesus every knee should bow, of things in
heaven, and things in earth, and things under earth;
And that every tongue should confess that
Jesus Christ is Lord, to the glory of God the Father.
–Philippians 2:9–11

E xcited that another Friday had graced the calendar, I
eagerly began my morning routine knowing I could
tackle anything that came my way. On that Friday, I
had plans to join friends at the campus dining hall for break-

fast. Beginning a Friday with food, friends, and fellowship was a perfect springboard for the upcoming weekend. When I arrived at the dining hall, I was greeted by the aroma of grease mixed with the smell of more grease. The words of a former coach forever ring in my ear, "To be early is to be on time and to be on time is to be late," which meant I was the first of my friends to arrive. As someone with limited vision, I always try to limit my visual field. Entering a large dining hall and trying to locate friends who were already seated would have been an arduous task and a potentially awkward scenario since I would have had to take the scenic route to the appropriate table. Arriving early had its advantages since I could stand by the main entrance where everyone had to enter to scan their student ID. As my mind relaxed knowing I was the first to arrive, my focus quickly turned to not looking lost as I loitered next to the entrance. I could have simply acted like a morning greeter, but I decided it would be normal to aimlessly scroll through my phone while I endured the wait.

After a brief time of waiting, I was approached by my friends, and we entered the dining hall together to obtain nourishment for the day. My taste buds were calling out for a fresh, warm waffle, but that would come with the risk of making a mess or creating a line at the waffle maker. Reluctantly I went with the premade hot cakes as my main entrée. With a complete tray of breakfast items, I carefully followed my friends to an open table.

I sat down and had my fork in hand when my friend exclaimed with enthusiasm, "Hey, Kurt! You like chocolate syrup on your pancakes as well?"

Stunned and faced with the reality that I didn't have maple syrup on my pancakes, I quickly replied, "Yeah, it's not a bad option, is it?" Let me clarify, chocolate has its place in the world of pancakes, but only in the form of chips. As enlightening and invigorating conversation took place, I tried my best to force down life's driest double stack. While this did start my day with a minor setback, it couldn't dampen what was planned to be an enjoyable day. Glancing at my watch, I noticed it was approximately twenty minutes until my 9 a.m. sport's management class. I noted this aloud, and we all decided it was time to move on with the day's activities.

Reaching my desired front-row seat in the classroom, I opened my backpack to pull out my necessary materials for lecture. Simultaneously, I noticed the volume level inside the room was lower than usual. Because the class was so early, I guessed that many students probably had made the quick transition from their places of slumber.

But I could not have been more wrong on this occasion.

I started chatting with a team member of our women's basketball team for which I was a student manager, and she immediately asked if I was ready for the exam. Unlike the earlier pancake incident, my response was much more on point and accompanied with slight anxiety.

"Wait a second, there is an exam this morning?"

"Yes, you studied, right?"

Of course, I wanted to believe that this was just a joke or a misunderstanding, but I could already feel the rush of panic overcoming my brain. I was suddenly going to be faced with an exam that I had not prepared for—obviously one that I had overlooked.

Rationalizing this oversight, I tried to convince myself that I could do a quick glance through my binder. Under increasing mental panic, I tried to use the remaining moments before class to inject as much information as possible into my brain. In what seemed like just a snap of the fingers, the instructor entered the room and closed the door—or in my mind, the barricade.

Could it be that there would be a change in schedule? Could it be that the test would be minimal in complexity? Could I suddenly come down with a bad stomachache after a blind man's misjudgment in the dining hall?

The first one seemed unlikely and the third would require quick action, so I was willing to hang my hope on the second. Surely, with this course centered on my major area of study I could find a way to play through the lack of preparation. Developing a slight bump in confidence, I listened as the announcements were displayed on the screen. Keeping a sharp ear to listen, I followed along with each bullet point and every passing word—that was, until the final announcement, which was to pull everything off the desk except a writing utensil and a blue book. Internally, I exclaimed, "Blue book!" Clearly my lack of preparation was going to be revealed. Not having purchased a blue book from the student union, I would have to ask around for one or hope the professor had a few extra.

As the exam sheets were being distributed, I asked the instructor, "Do you happen to have any extra blue books?"

She paused a moment and then said, "I can find you one."

Only slightly relieved, I turned focus to the type of test I was facing. Blue books only meant one thing: an extensive amount of writing. There was no falling back on the odds that true or false questions offered, not even the slightly worse odds of the multiple-choice format. This test was going to require concrete knowledge, thought, and explanation. Clearly the second option had failed me … I wondered if there was still time for an emergency exit to the safe walls of the men's room. The time had come to face the test, and my lack of preparation was squarely weighing on my shoulders.

Have you ever encountered a test you were not prepared for or even could not have anticipated? Advancing into a test unprepared isn't a welcoming feeling; it is one that leaves us vulnerable.

Life will place tests in your path that are anticipated, but it will also place many you would have never envisioned. Knowing that we can expect tests to arise, why wouldn't we prepare ourselves?

Christ himself completed the greatest test in human history at calvary. Christ who knew no sin became sin for the entire world and for all generations. He willingly stepped from the throne and in flesh accepted the test to shed His blood for the world's iniquities so that we could enter a personal relationship with him. As a believer who has put their faith and trust in Jesus Christ, no test will be faced alone. Faith in God alone means a place to shelter, a place to find hope, and a place to regain strength.

Consider how God created you entirely for the purpose of a close relationship with Him. Now imagine His pain and disappointment as God looks upon humanity struggling and fighting day and night to make a way. He yearns to deliver us, He desires to be the one who sticks closer than a brother, and He wants to be our first love. When we link ourselves to God, there is no test on this side of heaven that cannot be overcome.

Academically, we prepare for tests by reading, memorizing, and establishing foundational points. A popular way to study involves index cards on which information is recorded in an abbreviated form. This technique is not only sufficient for recalling information but also visually brings critical points in focus. You have heard that a proper sermon must have three points. While we all know that isn't true, I identified three critical words that have changed my everyday approach to life. These words are not only linked to my name and journey, but more importantly, they are linked to the Name Above All Names.

In the way a response is necessary in the classroom, a response is necessary in life. With varying degrees, life will present tests, challenges, and storms that give us a multitude of emotions. It's never wrong to experience these emotions, but our response can be out of line if we only act from our emotions. Living a life centered around God, we can have a response that reflects our dependence and unwavering faith. Through every life challenge, I've held these three words in my mind: praise, pray, and persevere. These words have become my response and my daily commitment to leading a life that is acceptable before a holy God.

Creativity is a special gift, one that remains hidden for so many. In fact, you likely know someone with the gift of creativity. I encourage you to use your creativity to develop your own strategy. Inspirational messages can be found in schools, in locker rooms, on public signs, and in various other visible locations. Creating a message, a life statement, or a set of words designed specifically for your journey is powerful. It would simply be inappropriate for me to lay a claim of creativity for my words, but I am laying a claim of the importance they hold in my journey. I implore you to locate an index card or make a note in your mobile device to begin creating your personalized message. Claim a message for yourself that prepares you, delivers a positive response to life, and provides confidence in the journey God has designated for you.

Chapter 19

THROUGH PRAISE

Because thy lovingkindness is better than life,
my lips shall praise thee. Thus will I bless thee while I live:
I will lift up my hands in thy name.
–Psalms 63:3–4

Consistency is something everyone wants to have upheld daily. Granted, surprises or a change of pace can be a breath of fresh air, but most of us want consistency, specifically with good health, stable income, and living space. Yet, no one would stand in the way of an increase in any of those three areas, but to that point, it is feasible that a decrease can also occur. With that understanding, many people want to hold tight to the security of having their needs met continually. And while we are busy holding tight to health, income, and earthly possessions, do we ever stop to consider God's perspective? Is it wrong to want those areas to be fulfilled?

Absolutely not.

In fact, God wants to bless us and be our Provider. We see in His Word that He has plans for us to prosper. Under examination and self-reflection, where can our consistency be found? Is it possible that we are sometimes driven by emotion and the swirling winds of this life? It would be hard for you to point to one area in which you demonstrate consistency before God and for God.

When you are born and raised in the state of Indiana, you learn how to tie your sneakers sooner than any other kid across this great country. For basketball is not only a season; it is the fabric of life, an expression revealed from one driveway to the next across the Hoosier state. Lacing up a pair of sneakers and picking up a basketball is the fastest way to create happiness. It is inside of that happiness that a vision is born for many young girls and boys. Eyes are set on an opportunity to pull on the jersey of their local high school and compete on the hardwood in front of a packed gymnasium. Just the thought of being one of the five sitting on the bench, looking into a tunnel of team-mates, waiting to hear your name growled over the speakers was enough to get a kid excited. Like many others, I wanted to be a part of Indiana basketball. During my fifth-grade year, I moved to New Castle, home to the world's largest high school fieldhouse, and located just west of the New Castle Chrysler

High School Fieldhouse is the Indiana High School Basketball Hall of Fame. This was, and is, truly the big stage for high school hoops.

Recalling my first visit to the fieldhouse, I remember walking around the upper track that surrounded the seating bowl in complete awe. I hoped for an opportunity to be a part of New Castle Trojan Basketball in the future, but it was not in the cards for me.

With Molteno tubes in both eyes, physicians recommended I sustain from all contact sports. Receiving a hit to the eye during competition could result in damage to the tubes—and a further loss of vision. Recognizing my condition and inability to compete, I knew another avenue would be necessary for me to join the sports arena. It was during my middle school years that I began volunteering as a student manager for basketball, football, and even wrestling for a season.

From day one of football, I embraced my role and strived to better myself each practice. When I transitioned to ninth grade and became a freshman in high school, I continued my duties as a football manager, but due to my involvement with the band, I was expected to play on basketball game nights, meaning I would be in the stands and not behind the bench for the first time in a couple seasons. To classify this as agony would undersell my true feelings on game nights, so this is truly where my selling capabilities manifested.

The curriculum at my high school required a minimum of one year of music and one year of a selected foreign language. Both requirements were being fulfilled for me with Spanish and band. I desperately wanted to bring an end to both courses at the end of my freshman year, but my mom said that I could only drop one. Let me tell you, there is more than one way to lose sleep as a high school boy, and it doesn't always revolve around a high school crush. I knew there had to be a way to sell mom on allowing me to drop Spanish *and* pursue being a basketball manager instead of being in the band. Through two top-level selling mechanisms—persistence and begging—I finally closed the deal on dropping both activities my sophomore year. This was exactly the win that I needed, a transition that would forever teach me the importance of consistency.

I went to one of my best friends, who played on the basketball team, and asked if he could speak to the coach on my behalf and convince him that I could be a valuable asset as a manager. I provided a written note that was to be delivered to the coach asking for a chance to be a New Castle Trojan. In response, Coach Steve Bennett asked that I come to his office to meet him and talk about my request. I still remember walking up to the coach's door and seeing it slightly cracked open. I was incredibly nervous as I knocked and slightly pushed open the door to look in. Thankfully, Coach was at his desk and looked up to greet me. Remembering myself, I stated my name and that I would like to help as a basketball manager. I was expecting a long response or a list of questions, but he was very pointed with his response: "Kurt, are you able to be fully committed and consistently work hard?"

Of course, he could have asked me anything and my response would have been a resounding "yes!" The thrill of knowing that I could be a part of New Castle Basketball was overwhelming. At the time, the team was in preseason mode, also known as open gym. Thus began three years as the basketball manager at New Castle, an unforgettable journey.

All positions aside, if your feet were standing on the parquet floor of the fieldhouse, you had to be fully committed each day. When consistency was not evident in your effort, in your work, and in your attitude, you would be exposed. Accepting this coaching mentality was the structure I needed. Granted, I was not down on the block, running the point, or being implored to be physical on defense, but the importance of my work was the same. In 2006, this commitment was rewarded when we won the state championship against Jay County.

That moment in time was and remains incredibly special, but it was only for a season, and it was only a moment. Life is a collection of moments and seasons; how we respond to each determines our tomorrow. Like basketball, life's journey as a follower of Christ needs to display consistency. Make a declaration that your consistency is going to be rooted in your praise!

Why Praise?
The God who is on the mountain is the same God who is in the valley. Praise is not situational; praise is for every single day. Train your mind to focus on praise and thanksgiving. Let no space be created between your position and your praise, for your position is set in Christ. The first of my three Ps is praise. Let's reveal the reason for our praise, how we can praise, and the results of praise.

Reason for Praise

A command (Psalms 150:6)—The book of Psalms ends by commanding us to praise the Lord. In fact, we discover this is not limited to humanity only but everything that hath breath. That means all creation is commanded to bring praise to the Lord. Both of my eyes have been ravaged by congenital glaucoma, but I am still breathing. As my days continue, so will my praise!

God's greatness (Psalms 145:3)—Great is the Lord and deserving of praise! Looking into verse three of Psalms 145, we see the word "unsearchable" used. That does not indicate we cannot find God's greatness but that greatness is endless or cannot be quantified. I had the pleasure of visiting Yellowstone National Park, and the term that comes to mind is "vast." This is exactly how I think of God's greatness; even with a telescope, we can only see a small portion of God's work. But His greatness never interferes with His deep care for us. Often, we see individuals who claim greatness, status, and a platform in this life, yet their compassion wanes. God remains unchanged, and the warmth of His care is reason enough to praise.

God is worthy (Revelation 4:11)—The Lord is worth of receiving glory, honor, and power because He is creator of all things specifically for our pleasure. This leads me to think about the beauty of his creation and everything that surrounds us on this earth. As I was fishing one autumn evening, I looked around at God's endless beauty. Even through clouded vision, I could marvel in the colors, the smell of fall, and the gentle yet cool breeze across the water. One limitation, one disability, would not prevent me from experiencing God's greatness.

Meditating on his greatness produces the understanding that we can never fathom or fully appreciate how magnificent God is. Our King, the Highest Priest, is worthy!

Access to God (Psalms 100:4)—Four remarkably simple yet powerful words lead verse four. We are told to enter His gates through praise with a thankful spirit and that we have direct access to God. At eleven years old, I began to take an interest in NASCAR racing. I was drawn to Jeff Gordon as my favorite driver. Visually, his car was one of the easiest to see in the field. Whether it was the rainbow warriors' paint or the sharp look of flames, I could find it. The thrill of a Saturday night or Sunday win on the track for the twenty-four team was exactly what I loved to cheer for. I would praise him for the outstanding run, and I would be thankful for his success, but that did not give me personal access to my driver. Starting in 2000, each year I would make a summer trip to the Indianapolis Motor Speedway for the annual Brickyard 400. I vividly recall squeezing my fingers through the chain link fence watching the garage area, hoping to get a glimpse of Gordon. I would think about how I could get a "yellow shirt worker" (security) to give me access to Jeff Gordon for just five seconds. Jeff Gordon had a Hall of Fame career on the track and continues to be a terrific ambassador for the sport. Recently I had the honor and pleasure of meeting Jeff Gordon in person—but it took me over fifteen years to have access to my favorite driver for a few moments. As Christians, we always have access to the Highest One in all seasons.

Way of redemption (Ephesians 1:7)—We have redemption through His blood and the forgiveness of our sins in accordance with the riches of God's grace. Our God stepped down from the throne to become man for the sole purpose of taking on the weight of sin and dying upon the cross. Without the cross—without the shedding of blood—forgiveness and remission of sins would not be possible. Praise Him for the grace He showed to all humanity.

How to Praise

Lifting of hands (Psalms 63:4)—The two life verses that I hold in my heart are Psalms 63:3–4, which focus on the Lord's lovingkindness that is better than life itself; therefore, our praise is demonstrated by the lifting of hands. Never should we cross our arms when speaking of the Lord. Willing and able, our hands should be ready to stretch forth and motion to the source of true love.

Words (Psalms 9:1)—My level of confidence is high when I say that I have never been told to speak up. This refers to volume, but it also refers to the fact that the audience needs to hear your message. When praising God for His marvelous works in your life, speak up! The audience is the world; let them know what God has done for you. Giving credit to luck, chance, good fortune, or a claim that the stars aligned is not praise. Be glad and find it comforting to share these blessings in spoken words. May your speech be a steady stream of praise, one that is like a natural spring that forever brings forth refreshing words of praise.

In fellowship (Hebrews 2:12)—For those who have been sanctified, there is a fellowship between the believer and God. Wonderfully, this extends to all those who are sanctified for the scripture says we are all of one and should not be ashamed to call them brethren. Surrounding ourselves with fellowship that involves praise is one of the most empowering and special offerings we can give to God. I still remember my trip to the island of Palawan in the Philippines where I met a group of believers on a mission trip. Every element of life was different, but the common bond was our love for the Lord. Our first dinner together was filled with laughter and joy, anticipating the week of service to come in the local schools. Let our praise ring out in fellowship!

Singing (Psalms 100:2)—Come before His presence with singing! I will admit that the Lord did not bless me in the area of singing. When I have been asked to sing a solo, it is always so low that others cannot hear it. Despite levels of talent, music strikes a chord for so many, and it isn't a surprise that music is incorporated with praising God. In fact, we can expect there to be singing in heaven, so why shouldn't we warm up our vocal cords today?

Serving (John 13:34)—We are to love those around us as Christ first loved us. The answer to how we can do this can be found in Jesus' life as He lived to serve others and served the world's greatest need. To describe today's generation as self-serving would be an understatement. Philippians 2:4 is clear that we should look to others' interests, not just our personal interests. Thank goodness looking is not confined to the visual aspect; it also means to listen to others, seek others, and desire to be a blessing to others. A servant mentality brings joy to both parties and a value that enriches one's spirit. Praising God with your gifts, talents, and resources delivers on others' prayers. I have discovered countless times that my prayers were answered by the work of fellow believers who simply dedicated their lives to serving others. Never will you discover that God is limited; he wants to use the people in our lives to serve a great purpose. What better task could there be than one that is assigned from God himself? Through the service element of praise, God directs us to multiple opportunities where we are needed.

Results of Praise

Promotes productivity (Psalms 17:5-6)—Just because you are moving does not always mean you are moving forward. Have you ever considered that your praise can yield productivity? Let the Lord hear your praise, as He is the one who will hold up your goings and ensure your footsteps do not slip. I love that "goings" and "footsteps" are plural, being active and moving forward with praise on the tip of our tongue.

God will protect you (Psalms 5:11)—Shout for joy because God will defend you. Friend, there is no room for worrying about receiving protection in this life. God keeps those who put their trust in Him and rejoice in it safe. He provides an all-encompassing protection that reaches farther than any fence, security system, or device that can be created by man.

Changes our focus (Isaiah 61:3)—We see ourselves as less than Christ. Whether it be internal or external communication, our focus usually falls on ourselves. The biggest contributor to changing our attitude, outlook, and demeanor is shifting our focus from self to Christ. Far too many people choose to feel down on their luck or lay in a bed of sorrows. It takes consistency and training to convert our mind from pain and to praise. Even in the darkest portion of the night or driving rains of the storm, can your praise be heard? Just as Jesus was on the boat to calm the storm, He can bring light to your life. For the darkness can be unsettling and the storm can be powerful, but Christ will overcome them all. This is a call to change our mind and our focus and rely on the One who always delivers on His promises. Transfer your attention from the problem to praise.

Renews your spirit (Psalms 28:7)—From rejoicing in your heart with your song develops a renewing of the spirit. Each one of us needs to be reminded that God is our strength and our shield. Every day can look and feel like a battle. Questions of insufficiency, weakness, and resistance cloud our minds. Praise brings peace and a renewing of our spirit to reassure us that we are not alone.

Makes miracles possible (Acts16:25–26)—When Paul and Silas were in prison, they prayed and sang praises to God. In fact, it was loud enough that fellow prisoners heard them. During this praise, a great earthquake shook the foundation, all the doors were opened, and the bands of the prisoners were loosened. Is it possible that you find yourself in a position where you cannot find an escape? No matter which way you turn, how hard you reason, and the might you display, it is a lost cause. As Paul and Silas would testify, praise produced a miracle. God wants to do a mighty work on your behalf and for His glory. At the midnight hour, will your praise be heard?

152 THROUGH BLURRED VISION

Application

On occasion, I catch myself sitting behind the wheel of my Ford Mustang or F-150—at least, in my mind. Independence is something I have not been able to experience fully due to my inability to secure a valid driver's license. Even with corrective lenses, I cannot pass the vision portion of the driver's test. Not being able to hold my own set of keys has been a constant source of disappointment and aggravation. Since my sixteenth birthday, I've felt disconnected from a part of society, unable to freely operate as I desire. Finding alternative modes of transportation to the grocery store, pharmacy, or work can create challenges, yet the hardest part is not being able to be spontaneous in my plans and actions. What if I meet a young lady who catches my attention and I strike up a conversation with her? If I want to ask her out on a date, in the back of my mind, I know that I can't provide transportation or make it simple for her. Or sometimes I desperately want to serve other people by making a visit to a hospital, cooking a meal for a family, or anything that uses my energy for someone else. All such instances require the use of personal transportation to meet the desire or need. The boundaries and containment aren't feelings that I like to experience, but they have resulted in one of my greatest praise items.

Through the years, I have relied on friends, coworkers, church members, and other connections to get from place to place. Each connection has enabled me to feel the love other people carry in their hearts. God has used so many people as a blessing and often an answer to my prayers. Without my disability, these relationships would cease to exist. Try to determine the number of hours you spend in the car over the course of a week, a month, or even a year. The hours quickly add up, and each of those hours are shared with another individual in my case. As the miles are added to the speedometer, so is the love added to my life.

Does this mean I've overcome feeling disappointment or aggravation from time to time? Absolutely not. Human nature still kicks in, and I can be caught in the emotion of the moment. But responding in the moment of emotion with praise turns the script from a problem to praise. With a brief time of reflection and reconsideration, I am reminded of the blessing that has come from one of life's trials.

It is difficult for people to change their thoughts midstream in a moment of stress and anxiety. It's something none of us can uphold 100 percent of the time. Being transparent, we know that we fall short, but depending on the Lord for our strength is the right attitude. With that attitude and an effort to respond with praise, we can build a stronger testimony.

Outside of single moments, I am going to challenge you to ensure your praise is coming forth in a broader sense. Dedicate a notebook, a mobile note, or even a dry erase board to "Items of Praise." Right before crawling into bed, list three items of praise for the day or things you are thankful for. Be consistent with this practice for at least one month. This exercise is extremely beneficial for individuals, but I also encourage it as a family activity. There may be some overlap with your praise items but try to develop new praises as often as possible. Many of these praises might seem classified as minor but actually make a major impact in our lives.

With the ultimate conviction of being consistent in our praise, this method helps us remember to praise during pressure situations. When the vices of life press in, our praise comes out.

Chapter 20

THROUGH PRAYER

Be careful for nothing, but in everything by prayer
and supplication with thanksgiving let your requests
be made known unto God. And the peace of God,
which passeth all understanding, shall keep your hearts
and minds through Christ Jesus.
—Philippians 4:6–7

P ause is a word that is rarely used in today's fast-paced society, a word that makes people uncomfortable in the moment, and a word that has been misinterpreted to mean lack of production.

Remember when we would use VHS players? Primarily, we would hope that the video tape was already rewound and ready to play upon insertion. Along the front of the VHS player were several buttons, but the largest was the play button. I remember being so anxious to hammer that play button and start the movie; however, without fail, there was always a pause, whether that was before the movie to make a bowl of popcorn or during the movie for a bathroom break.

I did not like the pause; I wanted to hit play as soon as I could.

Before the scene selection function existed, we would also use the fast-forward button to jump to the start of the movie. Most people today want to hit the fast-forward button and move on to each task as quickly as possible. It's quite common for both parents to hold full-time jobs, sometimes even picking up a side hustle or secondary means of income, and kids are involved in a multitude of activities in and outside of school. Even we experience a few moments of pause, there is a sense of uneasiness. Our natural reaction is to reach for our phone to check email, send a text message, or scroll through various social media platforms.

We cannot handle pause. We avoid pause to the best of our ability.

Like with the VHS player, we need to break the habit of looking to press the play button as soon as possible. Pause and pray needs to be the new mindset.

When you rise in the morning, pray. When you are commuting to work, pray. When you are running lunch errands, pray. During work, yes, pray!

Develop a rich and fervent prayer life. Pray on the highest of highs and in the lowest of lows. At the moment your knees become achy, at the moment tears bead down your cheeks, at the moment your palms are sweaty ... you have barely begun. Do not confuse God's delay with denial; pray, pray again, pray some more, and pray without ceasing. The need is great, my friends. Pause and pray today!

Prayer is the avenue through which we have contact with God—contact with the Creator of the universe and the One who holds it all in the palm of His hand. Coming down from Glory, Jesus donned human flesh to accomplish the Father's will, and Jesus' life is characterized by prevailing prayer. This was not merely public communication but also personal actions. Jesus spent time with the children, Jesus spent time with the disciples, Jesus spent time teaching, and Jesus always spent time in prayer. We are focusing on the Son of Man, the only person to live a blameless and perfect life, yet this did not change the importance of prayer.

Jesus spent approximately three years in public ministry. We've all experienced the crunch of time limits and the shortness of days. Let us say we only had three years to accomplish the things we set out to do. How many of us would be allotting entire nights to fervent prayer? The number would be very few for a myriad of reasons (i.e., excuses).

When the disciples asked Jesus how they were to pray, He not only provided the Lord's Prayer but also provided lessons throughout all his passages. Jesus did not only speak to be the example; he lived to be the example. His words were not only spoken in public but also were lifted in private. How is your public word verses your private word? Is there a balance between them? Is it balanced because you participate in prevailing prayer, or is it balanced because you really don't pray at all? Prayer does not need proof; prayer only needs practice.

In fact, through praise in prayer, we align ourselves with spiritual awakening. Come to the throne room boldly with thanksgiving and heartfelt praise and lay your petitions before the feet of Christ. In the book of Isaiah, God tells us to command it. Do not approach each prayer with a question mark and hesitation. Pray expecting God to move on your behalf! Pray for the smallest of requests and pray for the requests that are impossible. Believing is the key word, along with receiving what God has revealed. Recall John 3:16, the most memorized verse in scripture. The keyword in that verse is "believing." Believing is how we see God move. Carry every aspect of your life in prayer and believe God will come through.

Jesus rightly balanced His public service and His private service. Everything has a place and time and there must be an order when it comes to prayer. When you are blessed with the opportunity to eat at a public restaurant and enjoy a meal, you should pray and give thanks for what you have and who you have, but I would not recommend an hour-long prayer before enjoying a lunch or dinner.

We are told to love our neighbors higher than ourselves. Entering a long prayer before eating may result in great pain for you considering that not everyone needs two forks to eat their meal. That second fork may become a weapon for the back of your hand during extended prayer while everyone is hungry.

But in all seriousness, prayer is the second of the three Ps that position us for higher living.

Pray in Faith (Hebrews 11:6)

Without faith, it is impossible to please God. Those who diligently seek him will be rewarded. There is absolutely no way around it; we must enter prayer through faith.

How do you pray in Faith?

Faith stands for: Full Assurance in the Heart.

For every second you spend in prayer, know with your whole heart that God not only hears you but also sees your heart. He waits for you to ask and is ready to intercede on your behalf. Rest assured that He is as close as the air escaping your mouth; He is ready to receive our spoken words. Praying in faith means praying in assurance.

Just as important as praying in faith is praying in submission. Far too often we point the finger at ourselves and say, "If I only had enough faith, the outcome would have been different." It is not right for us to place ourselves on the same level of importance as God. Within a small segment of time, it is impossible for us to understand and see the whole picture. Submission to God's will is irreplaceable in your prayer life. Without submission, discouragement can come and quite possibly kickstart a rebellion against God. Most of the time we have predetermined our desired outcome, but God orchestrates everything; He knows what we need and knows our purpose. Let us not forget that God can delay, God can answer prayer in an unusual way, and God may not give us exactly what we want.

Living in this earthly body, sometimes our requests can be self-serving. That's not to say that our desires are wrong. In fact, I would be the first person to tell you that God wants to bless us. Just as Jesus turned water into wine at the wedding feast, he offers us happiness and celebration. Blessings are at His right hand not only in eternal glory but for this life as well.

Expect the road to be tough and expect the journey to be long because God wants to not only test our faith but also strengthen it. He will take you through the fire, but you will not be burnt. He will take you through the waters, but you will not drown. He desires to mold us into the image of his Son.

Do we shudder at the sight of trouble? Do we cling to the safety of the harbor? Do we live with shackles on our feet that are bound by fear?

Our eyes, heart, and mind should be directed toward God and God alone. Prayer demands faith!

Pray in Righteousness (James 5:16)

Elijah was an ordinary man; he wasn't an extraordinary saint. He was simply a righteous man who placed importance on praying. One day Elijah bent down, placed his face between his knees, and began to pray. He asked his servant to look at the sea and determine if there were signs of incoming rain. Elijah did this seven times before his servant located a small cloud that had formed. Elijah was earnest in his prayer, but he was also consistent in his request. God showed favor to Elijah and brought forth rains to end the drought.

Do you find your life in a drought? Have you been asking for rain? Are you asking continually for blessings to rain down?

James 5:16 tells us to confess our sins to one another. Ask for forgiveness and show humility to those around you. Christ first forgave us, so who are we to withhold forgiveness from others? One of the simplest illustrations I can provide is yardwork during the summer when you need to mow the lawn, trim the hedges, and weed the yard. Throughout the day, sweat, dust, and grass clippings are going to collect on your clothes. Let's say at the end of the day, you go to bed without showering or changing clothes, but we would never actually go to bed without taking a shower. How many times do we bow our heads in prayer with unconfessed sin in our heart? Like taking a shower, we need to renew our minds every day and pray for forgiveness for the areas in which we fail. Other people's actions do not justify your actions. Every man and every woman must ask for forgiveness individually.

As I covered earlier in the book, one of my greatest struggles has been my relationship with my biological father. Years of turmoil, years of a reckless pursuit to bring pain, and years of not listening made it difficult to forgive him. I've since forgiven him and asked God to let me move forward with my life with no grudges toward my father. I've shared with my father that I forgave him, but he is unwilling to ask for forgiveness himself. But I have learned that I am only responsible for myself and for making sure that I have it set right before God. If I desire a productive prayer life, I must keep a soft heart and ask for forgiveness for any sin committed. Like dirt and grass clippings that collect on your clothes, so does sin without confession. For those who have accepted the perfect free gift of salvation, there is remission of sins; however, this does not mean that sin can't enter our lives. Unconfessed sin will absolutely bind us and impede every one of our prayers.

The verse continues in James 5:16 with "and pray for one another." God finding us righteous not only determines our effectiveness in prayer for ourselves but also our effectiveness in prayer for other people. More than ever, we need righteous individuals praying in homes, praying in the church body, and praying throughout our land. By the way of our own murmurings and by the deception of Satan, we have lost the tenderhearted approach when it comes to confessing sin. But like Elijah, any ordinary person like us can become a righteous person.

Pray in Everything (1 Thessalonians 5:17)

Although one of the shortest verses in the Bible, we receive a commandment in 1 Thessalonians 5:17 to "pray without ceasing." This means there should be no end to our prayers. The answer to how often a person should pray is straightforward: continually.

At the beginning of this chapter, I highlight the word "pause" as it pertains to the need to pause and pray when society wants to press the "play" button repeatedly. It's perfectly acceptable for prayer not to be interrupted as referenced in 1 Thessalonians 5:17. In the Bible, Abraham continued to pray, and as he continued to pray, God did not bring destruction upon the City of Sodom nor harm to Lot. Living in a fast-paced society, I can only imagine the lack of commitment when it comes to prayer. I don't wish to take a negative tone; this is simply the message that our world sends out repeatedly. The coronavirus pandemic has been extremely difficult on people around the entire globe. Hopefully, we begin to hear more testimonies of those who committed to regular prayer during this time. I would encourage you to find prayer partners who can hold you accountable. Absorb the joy of praying for one another and engaging in fellowship with each other and with God.

Finally, make plans for private prayer. The Bible speaks of having a prayer closet, a place to do business with God, although truthfully, it is more of a place where God does business with us. Prayer is not getting God prepared to do your will; prayer is getting you prepared to do God's will. Grab the quilt from the back of the sofa and lay it down to protect your knees as you pray before an almighty God. If you are married and/or have kids, create a private space where you can escape to spend time in diligent prayer. Although prayer can be conducted on a boat, an escape to the fishing boat does not count as your prayer closet. It's not the private space that you need for adequate prayer.

Jesus prayed through an entire night, and Jesus rose early to pray in the morning so that He was alone. Allocate time to pull yourself away from the hustle and bustle of life for the purpose of prayer. In this practice, we can expect the peace of God that surpasses all understanding, and it shall keep our hearts and minds. Through prayer, we have a heavenly Father who will make our paths straight.

Chapter 21

THROUGH PERSEVERANCE

I press toward the mark for the prize
of the high calling of God in Christ Jesus.
–Philippines 3:14

Perseverance is the last of the three Ps. Through perseverance, we can reach the heavenly hope promised to us.

I've never had to look far to see an example of perseverance and resilience. My mom has certainly operated with a great deal of tenacity and grit to overcome the towering obstacles that were placed in her path. I treasure the times we have shared genuine and profound conversations about our past. The fight she exhibited as an individual is admirable when even her own mother and father labeled her as a child abuser for seeking medical intervention. Mom's journey is best described in two words: press on!

My visual impairment could have been an excuse for relaxed boundaries because of her sympathy for me. My mom is very compassionate, but she made perseverance her stronghold. She recognized that being knocked down is okay but staying down is unacceptable.

Unequivocally, perseverance is a mainstay in my life. I could have chosen to relinquish the fight and accept defeat many times. Opportunities came from many angles, crushing me at the core to the point where I did not know if I could be remade. The keyword here is "I," for if indeed it was "I," then I could not be reassembled. My hopeless attempt at reconstruction would result in a horrifying picture. Thank goodness God has control of my life. I give full responsibility to Him to reassemble the pieces and make a new work through His power. Praise God I can stand on the rock and say that when I've been down, God has been up working. As I was being crushed, I was being remade. Hallelujah that when I was locked in waiting, God was making a new schedule.

Do not ever try to put limits or restrictions on God. We humans like to structure our time and stick to a precise agenda. God is the keeper of time, and He orchestrates time on his watch. Expect God to adjust the timing in your life. Just because things do not look the way you assumed they would does not mean you should give up. Do not rob yourself of the abundant blessings God is ready to pour into your life. A process is in place; let your perseverance lead you to the amazing plan that God has created specifically for you. We do this by persevering for the prize, persevering for the again, and persevering for the victory.

Persevere for the Prize (Philippines 3:14)—We focus on our forward momentum, refusing to look behind us since the prize lies before us. We cannot be distracted by what has transpired in the past. Far too often we allow yesterday's faults to interfere with tomorrow's focus. As Paul explains in the Bible, the runner needs to have complete focus on the prize ahead. Our prize as Christians is an eternal home in heaven with Jesus Christ.

Like a runner presses toward the finish line, so should we press toward the finish line in our own life. This is the high calling in Christ Jesus as we are on the path to meet the One who died for all the sins of the world.

Jesus Christ endured through the end; He could have escaped the pain and suffering on the cross, but He remained, willingly taking on the sin and shame for every single man and woman because of his infinite love for each soul.

I press on because I want to meet the One who died for me. I press on because I want to meet the One who gave me hope when there was no hope. I press on because I want to meet the One who gave me joy when there was no joy. I press on to meet the One who is preparing a place for me. I press on to bow before the King.

Perseverance becomes much more manageable when we visualize our reason for running the race. The prize isn't a medal, a check, or a trophy; it is to reside with the One who loved me first.

Even before bearing the cross, Jesus knew my faults and that I would disappoint Him, yet that did not stop Him from shedding his precious blood for the remission of sins. Ceremonies are typically conducted to reward individuals after an occasion, but Christ rewarded us first, all the while knowing that man would fail Him once again. So, press on, endure to the end, and persevere because we are headed for glory!

Persevere for the Again (Proverbs 24:16)—We are not promised a perfect or easy life in scriptures. The promise is for a faithful God who will never leave us nor forsake us. God has His hand placed upon the righteous. For though the righteous fall seven times, they rise again! Proverbs 24:16 is the perfect representation of resiliency through the word "again." The righteous will rise again, but the wicked will be consumed with calamity. Knowing that even the righteous will fall, we expect that trouble will come. Our hope is not rooted in this life; our hope is found in our Father's plan for us and in Jesus Christ. We know the trials of this life are temporary; therefore, we rise again and again and again and persevere through every trial.

So many individuals are consumed with the success of this life and providing a status update on social media. Those who do not know God and are spending their life collecting goods will be extremely disappointed and angry when tough times come. The word "again" is connected to getting up because we are not damaged when we live in the eternal promise from God. Circumstances will change, location will change, and finances will change, but God never changes. We rise again after tough times with gratitude in our heart, thanking God for the trial.

This is where living with congenital glaucoma becomes a gift for me. I thank God for all the inconvenient situations I would have never experienced if I did not have a visual impairment. This journey is truly a unique gift from God. I find it a joy to persevere, to rise again knowing my limited sight is shaping new vision. God allows the invasion of difficulties to develop us, not to destroy us. I love the illustration of a palm tree during a storm for this. The tree may be held to the ground during hurricane winds, but as soon as the storm passes, the tree rises again and stretches its palms. That's the image you can hold onto: rise and stretch forth your hand toward God in praise. We are God's workmanship, and He is constantly creating enduring faith through the storms. He will not send more than you can bear; He trusts you to respond in faith and rise again. God is counting on you to persevere!

Persevere for the Victory (Galatians 6:9)—As we press toward the prize and rise repeatedly, the flesh can become weary, and we can start to wonder if this race is worth it. Paul tells Christians that they cannot respond to the flesh and trust impulses that arise; he preached that they must remain steadfast in their beliefs and reminded them that God's spirit was with them. Galatians 6:9 tells us that we must not grow weary because in due season we shall reap.

Perseverance is directly connected to the harvest we expect. I like to think of the harvest as the promised reward. At all times, our mind must be focused on the eternal victory that awaits us. Abstain from growing weary while staying the course; you have already been guaranteed victory. Don't give up, and certainly don't give into the flesh. God's power is inside of you. It will make it so that you can persevere. God will not only bless us with eternal fruit but also will bless us with fruit in this life when we invest properly through good matters. Whether we realize it or not, those around us are watching how we respond to life. When you experience adverse circumstances, you better believe people will be watching with even greater interest. As I emphasize in the next chapter, we can trust in the Savior, scriptures, and service that guarantee a harvest. Through perseverance in doing good, we can—and we will—succeed.

At this very moment, you have everything you need to persevere. Do not waste time creating a list of things that you don't have or elements you are waiting for. God has given you exactly what you need to press on. Nothing is impossible for you. Claim the power you have been granted through His Word. God will not withhold any good thing from those who diligently seek Him, so seek Him!

Never have we been offered more resources related to God's Word than we are today. Maybe you are having trouble because your devotion to the Word isn't what it needs to be. Perseverance means we hold God's Word in our hearts and know that God communes with us. The truth of your testimony is tested in trouble.

In 2 Corinthians 4:8–9, the Bible lets us know that there will be pressure. We will be perplexed but not in despair. Through perseverance, we hold onto the same hand who went with the three Hebrew children through the fire. Stick with God, press on, and train your heart to be anxious for nothing.

Chapter 22

BUILT IN TRUST

And be not conformed to this world: but be ye transformed
by the renewing of your mind, that ye may prove what is
that good, and acceptable, and perfect, will of God.
–Romans 12:2

P raise, prayer, and perseverance are biblical mechanisms that promote higher living; however, if trust
is not embedded in your daily journey, the three Ps
are insufficient—specifically trust in the Lord, not an empty
trust that circumstances will play out. Proverbs 3:5 states it
best: "Trust in the Lord with all your heart." Trust also can
be read as believe in—believe in the Lord with all your heart.

Believing in something bigger than yourself is an inspirational phrase used for moments of motivation. What could be bigger than believing in the one and only true God? Trust in the One who has overcome life and death and reigns on the most high.

Honestly, it is hard to fully grasp the all-encompassing power of God and just how vast He is. To merely scratch the surface of how magnificent God is requires us to transform our minds every day.

Mornings are the best time of day to transform our minds. Mornings signify the blessing of a new day, an open opportunity; they should be the best part of any Christian's life. Whether your mornings start at 5 a.m. or 8 a.m., we should all be morning people. I realize that everyone is created differently. For some of us it may take longer for our tails to become bushy in the morning. Personally, I am astonished that some people can place their feet on the floor in the morning and immediately flip a switch to high energy. Let's be real, there is typically at least a thirty-minute activation period to the system. Many people need a line item in their budget for coffee just to ensure you can meet the day. But regardless of how long it takes you to get moving, mornings are important.

When I teach the teens Sunday school class, I often emphasize the importance of mornings because this time of day sets the tone for events throughout the rest of the day. We are saved by God's grace, but we also continue to live in the flesh. Our spirit is sealed forever more, but we are tempted in the flesh daily.

In Romans 12:2, the keyword "renewing" is used to describe what we do to our minds. In a recent study focused on leaving a legacy, one of the most tangible practices for doing so was renewing your mind every morning. The mind and the heart are closely connected; what we put in is ultimately going to come out. Without recognition or even permission, we are continually absorbing messages from the world around us. This ought to motivate us to better control what we are absorbing through our ears and our eyes; otherwise, we will be conformed to this world. By transforming our mornings and minds to include inputs from God's Word, we can change our outputs.

I believe the root of discouragement and complacency is failure. Each and every one of us has missteps, failures, and ill-advised decisions. Regardless of the length of your relationship with Christ, it will never be automatic to live a holy and separated life. This doesn't provide an excuse to give up but should make us recognize that renewing our mind each morning is vital. Renewing our mind in the morning helps us focus on things above and provides a springboard to transform the way we operate throughout the day.

Higher living awaits when we follow the right and perfect will of God because His ways are far higher than our ways. His thoughts are higher than our thoughts. Most certainly His love is higher than our love. God has authority through his Holy Word and waits anxiously for us to come to him. The password to renewing your mind daily is trust. The entire Christian walk is built upon trust—taking the complete Word of God and trusting every Word as it is written. We trust in the Savior, we trust in the scriptures, and we trust in the service. When you wake up each morning, ensure that you step forward only in trust.

What Do We Trust In?

Trust in the Savior (Proverbs 3:5–6)—Trust the savior daily in all your steps and in all your ways. Know that He is God, and He will absolutely supply every one of your needs. He will never separate Himself from us. No matter how things appear, don't turn your face from Him. I can't help but think about how many times people miss out on God's blessings simply because they throw in the towel. Hold tight to your salvation experience and relive it when you start to feel weak. Make the experience fresh again in your mind and go back to the point of salvation when your burdens were lifted forever. Humbling your heart before His feet, you trusted Him with your soul for eternity. The rest of your Christian walk demands that same amount of trust continually.

Trust in the Scriptures (2 Timothy 3:16–17)—Notice that verse sixteen starts with the word "All," meaning that all scripture is from the inspiration of God. When we place our trust in all scripture, we see that the Word is profitable for doctrine, for reproof, for correction, and for instruction in righteousness. Skipping ahead to verse seventeen, we see that we are thoroughly furnished through scripture for all good works. Leaving any part of the scripture out prevents us from being thoroughly furnished. We need the complete truth before our eyes, trusting the scriptures in our hearts. It has become increasingly hard to locate a Bible in a public setting, and this has also become true in our homes. Does your Bible hold a place on the shelf, or does it hold a place in your day?

Trust in the Service (Philippians 2:3)—Over and over again we see a call to service. You cannot read scripture without seeing that love of others is required. Diligently serving those around you is one of the most important things you can do. Invest in the relationships that God has given you. Philippians 2:3 makes it clear that we are to value others more than ourselves, and according to 1 John 4:11, God loved us, and we must love one another. Sow the seed of love continually! Don't just take time or try to find time but schedule time to invest in others' lives. We enter this world with nothing, and we will leave this world with nothing. I absolutely love this quote from Denzel Washington: "You will never see a U-Haul following a hearse." We cannot physically take anything with us, but as Christians, we can leave a legacy.

Too many of us prefer to use money or words alone to help people because that is most efficient when we are asked for a lifetime of dedicated service. Learn someone's story, discover what they enjoy, partner with them in prayer, and be present to shoulder their care. We have a habit of pointing our fingers for direction, but we need to stop pointing fingers unless we are pointing at ourselves. Make it your responsibility to reflect Christ's love wherever you go. Proceed with the intention to resonate genuine love from your soul with every encounter. Through service to others, our blessings multiply while also depending on the Lord to use us as a blessing for others.

Renew your mind every morning and make certain that your trust is in the Savior, scriptures, and service. For those who have families, I realize this becomes increasingly difficult. In fact, the mornings can be the most challenging part of the day. Nevertheless, it is vital to make time to renew your mind.

Living the Christian life is flipping a switch that makes everything become automatic. I'm here to tell you that things become exceedingly difficult because your faith is going to be tested on multiple occasions. How are we supposed to be successful in our praise, in our prayer life, and in our perseverance if we do not commit to renewal? That foundation cannot be firm when trust is absent. Abandoning the personal time in the morning when we can reset our trust and focus has a negative affect across all spectrums of life. Your attitude will slip, your professional standards will be manipulated, your marriage will increase in selfishness, and you will accomplish what the enemy (Satan) wants: defeat. We cannot sacrifice our time with the Lord, but it is easy to revert to carnal ways because we still reside in human flesh and a world consumed with sin. Guard your heart, mind, and soul against all attacks by building trust and renewing your mind every morning.

Chapter 23

BLURRED VISION

Behold, I was shapen in iniquity;
and in sin did my mother conceive me.
–Psalms 51:5

According to a 2015 report from the Center for Disease Control and Prevention, 1.02 million people were blind and approximately 3.22 million were living with a visual impairment in the United States. Projections are that by the year 2050, both of those categories will double. Meanwhile, an earlier report from 2010 released numbers from the World Health Organization that recorded 285 million living with a visual impairment and thirty-nine million experiencing complete blindness. Glaucoma ranks fourth on the list of leading causes for visual impairment and/or blindness. The top three contributors are macular degeneration, cataracts, and diabetic retinopathy. In addition, during 2010, the economic burden of medical intervention was calculated to be three trillion dollars. Each case not only presents a physical difficulty but also financial weight. Over 50 percent of reported cases are connected to individuals who are sixty-four and over. Knowing these statistics allows us to understand the depths of the challenge and its heavy burden. Most people had near normal vision prior to their decline and diagnosis, and going through a time of deterioration in vision alters people's lives forever. Countless grasp for hope of blurred vision, desperate to maintain a fragment of sight.

As I mentioned earlier in the book, I was diagnosed only four days after birth with congenital glaucoma. This phenomenon only occurs in one infant per 10,000 births. Excellent care and medical intervention were provided within the first week of my birth, yet the damage was still severe. To date, I've had forty eye operations to salvage as much vision as possible. Currently my visual acuity is 20/80 in the right eye and 20/200 in the left eye—and those numbers are with the assistance of prescription glasses. Without the assistance of glasses, my entire world becomes completely blurry. Glaucoma causes a narrowing of the visual field, meaning that my peripheral sight is all but gone at this point in my life.

Imagine you are sitting around a campfire with some friends, and you so happen to be sitting in the direct line of the smoke. Trying to be funny, you grab the center roll from the paper towels and place it to your eye as a telescope. When you look through the cardboard tube, you can only see a limited area, and that area has taken on a distorted view due to the smoke in the air. This is the best representation of what I see on a daily basis.

Through blurred vision, I've come to experience life in a unique and altered perspective. History and medical records confirm my condition is rare, and there is no genetic evidence to explain my diagnosis. Through conversations with physicians, low-vision specialists, educators, and family, no one could provide an answer as to why. It would be a complete falsehood if I said there were never days when anger surfaces about the empty answers about why I have my condition. Those moments continued even after I accepted the Lord as my personal Savior. A new life had been established, but the process was only beginning for me to understand the why.

This chapter, and really this whole book, is the direct and clear response about why my disability is meant for good and the plan God has for me.

Serving as Assistant Director for Athletic Tours and Ticket Operations at Indiana Athletics, I befriended the Director of Athletic Performance for men's basketball. God uses his faithful servants to serve a greater purpose, and the understanding that God orchestrates all encounters grants undeniable joy. In February of 2018, I approached this director with the idea of starting a prayer and bible study group for fellow staff members. Many times it was just us two who would meet on Mondays during lunch for thirty minutes to read from a devotional and pray. One Monday he asked me to share my testimony. Through some investigative work and discussion on his part, he learned that I had tailored my testimony to fit my comfort level. Inside the walls of athletics, this director dedicates himself to strengthening men to play the game of basketball, but here he was strengthening my case for Christ. No one had ever demonstrated the level of care he took when coaching me to share my entire testimony. Right before Thanksgiving 2018, he invited me to speak with the men's basketball team during a voluntary chapel service before a home game and share it in its entirety for the first time.

Fast-forward to December 2019 when I made a list of twenty new things I wanted to do in 2020. Knowing that I've never experienced perfect vision as the year in itself suggested, I wanted to have perfect vision in my pursuit of good things that year. One of those items was writing my first book and sharing the why behind my diagnosis. Then the global pandemic reinforced my conviction to share as my friend encouraged.

While my visual condition is different from millions of people around the world, there is one common link that connects me to all 7.8 billion people around the globe. *Through Blurred Vision* highlights a battle with glaucoma, but it is all of mankind who enters the world with blurred vision because of sin. In Psalms 51:5, we understand that we were born into sin (darkness), and Romans 3:10 states that all have sinned. Let me expand upon this further by sharing a few verses from the book of Acts.

But rise, and stand upon thy feet: for I have appeared
unto thee for this purpose, to make thee a minister and a
witness both of these things which thou hast seen, and of
those things in the which I will appear unto thee; Delivering
thee from the people, and from the Gentiles, unto whom
now I send thee, To open their eyes, and to turn them from
darkness to light, and from the power of Satan unto God,
that they may receive forgiveness of sins, and inheritance
among them which are sanctified by faith that is in me.
–Acts 26:16–18

Here darkness and sin are referring to the same condition. Welcoming a precious soul is an unforgettable moment that we try to capture in every way possible, but we must realize that someone else is already at work trying to capture their soul. We see in the above verses from Acts the illustration of someone opening their eyes, as well as the word "turn" to describe a necessary action. What is it—or who is it—we need to turn from in order to have our eyes open to see the light? We must turn from Satan and the power of Satan.

In 1 Peter 5:8, notice Satan is described as a roaring lion, purposing to seek and destroy. Do you realize that Satan has a desire for your life? He wants to keep you bound by the chains of sin, confused in the darkness, and blind to the truth. But the greatness news is found in Jesus Christ and His perfect sacrifice for all the world. Through God's unmeasurable love, He stepped down from glory to conquer the darkness, to be the light, and to restore our vision. Society embraces the mentality that the more you work, the more you will be rewarded.

Friends, the work was completed on the cross, and your inheritance awaits. God's wants every man and woman to bow their hearts in humbleness and turn to Him. Look no further than Romans 10:9 to see how you can be pulled from the darkness into light.

> That if thou shalt confess with thy mouth the Lord Jesus, and shalt believe in thine heart that God hath raised him from the dead, thou shalt be saved.
> *—Romans 10:9*

Because of my visual impairment, I was brought outside during the night so that I could have the chance to open my eyes to the light from the moon and stars. Physically my condition was much different than most experience, but spiritually my condition aligns with all humanity. The affliction is lifted at the exact moment we discover that light originates from the Son of Man.

Without placing my complete dependence, hope, and life in God's hands, I tremble with fear considering where my journey could have gone. Knowing what I know today, there was ample opportunity for destruction and a life spent in darkness. My prayer and my plea are anchored in the hope that I can share truth with everyone who comes into my life. *Through Blurred Vision* is not only my testimony but also an incredible gift from God. Through peace of heart and gladness, he has unveiled the why in my life. Sharing in God's goodness and direction falls second to nothing. This book is my story, but really, it is God's story through me.

You have a purpose and a why in God's miraculous design. The story and the testimony may come in pieces—it truly is a process—but don't miss the first piece. Our vision is blurred until we recognize our personal need for a relationship with Christ.

Chapter 24

HURDLES IN THE RACE

Casting all your care upon him; for he careth for you.
–1 Peter 5:7

To compete well and to conquer the competition is the pulse of every athlete. Resistance is anticipated, but endurance is necessary for progress. The Apostle Paul had an athletic mindset in 1 Corinthians when he said that an athlete undergoes intense preparation to win the race. He then asks how many believers attack spirituality with the same mentality. In fact, attacking takes the form of denial in Paul's teachings—denying those things that are not good and do not support the mindset of running the race well.

Operating without discipline is counterproductive. It will not only damage your wellbeing but also that of those you share space with. Your placement, preparation, and performance effectively maintain your pace in life's race. Many claim they rely on their faith daily but are desperately hoping their faith will not be put to the test. Working to create comfort, we quickly construct walls that give us the illusion of safety and security. But no matter how hard we attempt security, the walls we construct will crumble when put to the test. When we suffer a major disruption, we cry out and become discouraged, all the while being completely foolish by building walls on the track instead of participating in the race.

Accepting the blood of Christ places our feet on the starting line but running begins when the runner steps forward. Is it possible that you are still standing at the start line? Did you make it one hundred, two hundred, or four hundred meters only to build walls?

The further you advance, the more tests will appear. To stick with the race comparison, these tests must be labeled hurdles. Let me share a personal quote that was placed on my heart at the onset of college.

> *There will be obstacles in your life.*
> *Never allow the obstacles to be a barrier;*
> *make them hurdles you will rise above.*
> –Kurt Pangborn

Determine that all obstacles will be hurdles you will rise above.

Dismiss all distractions and focus on your inner self and mind for these next few moments. As near as your next breath, your next heartbeat, and your next blink of an eye, there is also the Lord. For He can hear our very next thought, next word, and next conversation. In fact, He already knows everything about you and yearns for you to know His closeness. Partner with Him in every moment, every situation, and every hurdle.

I place my hands upon your shoulders as a friend, as a brother in Christ, sharing these words. Unapologetically, do whatever you need to do in order to believe this for yourself. Hearing the coach's shout, tighten up those laces, shift your eyes forward, and know that you can do this.

Expect the pains of running the race, expect to be pushed to your limits, but most of all, expect God to be your guide. Cast all your care upon Him; he cares for you. You are never alone and never overlooked. God is in the midst of your race. We are running the race because of God's amazing grace, endless love, and generous liberty through the presence of the Spirit.

Everyone must decide to either carry their cares or cast them. How many times do we squeeze our cares and hold them tightly to our chest out of pride and reluctance? Considering the comparison of running a race, it would be unthinkable to carry bricks in our arms while trying to run.

Maybe you fall into the group that has disguised their cares by placing the bricks into a backpack, hiding them in the innermost pockets, and throwing the bag over their shoulders with a smile. Storing away those bricks—those cares—will only add weight and stress to your journey.

Empty your cares upon the Lord. He awaits with open arms to catch your cares; we just need to turn them over to Him.

Sharing our wishes and desires can come naturally but sharing pain and anguish can be a great challenge. Even in my own walk, I was conditioned to keep quiet and push the hurt under the table. In days spent at school, practice, and church, no one had reason to believe that pain and disappointment lived on the walls of my heart. Like many others, I spent too many years trying to carry my own burdens and cares. Avoiding the hurt, emotion, and divide was my way of showing strength.

But this is not the Lord's way.

He has always been there, ready to catch my cares. Complete healing and peace came only when I transferred my cares into His hands.

If we have placed our faith and trust in the Lord Jesus Christ as our Savior for our eternal security, shouldn't we place that same faith and trust in Him to receive our cares in this life? You would think this to be an easy answer, but so many times we hold onto those cares and try to conquer them alone. God will overcome in all occasions and will illuminate a brighter future. Where there's a disability, He creates an ability. Where there's no earthly father, He is our heavenly Father. When there is devastation, He already knows the destination of victory. Hurdles are never intended to be barriers; they are elements used to elevate our faith.

Search your past, your cares, and the purpose for your life story. You fit perfectly into God's schedule. There will be no error found in his timing.

There was a time in my life when I envisioned playing the remarkable game of basketball. I was on the bench waiting for my name to be called for the starting five. As significant as that motivation was, there is a much bigger game to compete in now. Competing in life through praise, through prayer, and through perseverance overshadows any athletic scoreboard. There is simply no reason to wait, because the number of competitors is greater than five. In 2 Chronicles 16:9, God's eyes are searching for hearts devoted to him that want to serve.

Today is your day to step on the court of life and use your gifts for His glory.

Servants are needed in homes, servants are needed in the workplace, servants are needed in the community, and servants are needed across the world for the sake of the Gospel. Indeed, servants are needed on the mission field and behind the pulpit, but God's message of love and hope is meant for all industries and all people. Your place in this world is waiting! *Through Blurred Vision* we can all capture the light that comes from knowing the Son of Man and use it to transform lives.

CLAIM VICTORY

A thletics continues to be a main contributor in my life. From being a basketball manager at New Castle Chrysler High School to Vincennes University and Indiana University, the purpose was always victory. In my early days of participating in the local tee-ball league and being brought into games during middle school to kick field goals, the purpose was also victory. Working in collegiate athletics, we celebrate victories.

Sports are great teachers, and the thrill of victory is special for everyone who experiences it. Coaches, trainers, administrators, and support staff invest in the teams so that victory can be achieved. Winning on the field, court, or track is a testament to the investment prior to competition. Sharing my testimony is my attempt to invest in your life, and I want to be very direct about how you can claim victory in your life. The price has already been paid; it's up to you to accept the free gift of salvation. I discovered the true light of life and enjoy a personal relationship with my Lord and Savior Jesus Christ. The three Ps of praise, prayer, and perseverance cannot precede entering into a relationship with Christ. Remember, trust starts with the Savior. You do not need to put on the jersey as a starter, sit on the team bench, or even enter the stadium. There is an open invitation for everyone to claim victory right where you are!

The Path to Victory (God's Plan of Salvation)
Why do we need to be saved?

> For all have sinned and come short of the glory of God.
> *—Romans 3:23*

Sin is rebellion against God. Sin causes harm to us and our peers and ultimately dishonors God. God is holy and just; He cannot allow sin to go unpunished.

> For the wages of sin is death; but the gift of God
> is eternal life through Jesus Christ our Lord.
> *—Romans 6:23*

> And I saw a great white throne, and him that sat on it,
> from whose face the earth and the heaven fled away;
> and there was found no place for them. And I saw the
> dead, small and great, stand before God; and the books

were opened: and another book was opened, which is
the book of life: and the dead were judged out of those
things which were written in the books, according to their
works. And the sea gave up the dead which were in it;
and death and hell delivered up the dead which were in
them: and they were judged every man according to their
works. And death and hell were cast into the lake of fire.
This the second death. And whosoever was not found
written in the book of life was cast into the lake of fire.
—Revelations 20:11–15

When we don't accept Christ as our personal savior, we
bear our sin debt and are judged by our works. This judgment
sends us into an eternal separation from God in the lake of
fire. God is the only one who can provide salvation after He
became flesh in the form of Jesus Christ

In the beginning was the Word, and the Word
was with God, and the Word was God ... And the Word
was made flesh, and dwelt among us (and we beheld
his glory, the glory as of the only begotten
of the Father), full of grace and truth.
—John 1:1–14

Jesus lived a sinless life.

And ye know that he was manifested to take away
our sins; and in him is no sin.
—1 John 3:5

He offered himself as the perfect sacrifice.

By the which will we are sanctified through the offering
of the body of Jesus Christ once for all.
—Hebrews 10:10

Since Jesus is God, His death was of infinite and eternal value. The death of Jesus Christ on the cross fully paid for the sins of the entire world.

And he is the propitiation for our sins: and not
for ours only, but also for the sins of the whole world.
—1 John 2:2

His resurrection from the dead demonstrated that his sacrifice was sufficient, and that salvation is now available to all. How can we be saved? Paul was asked this very question in Acts 16:31.

And they said, believe on the Lord Jesus Christ,
and thou shalt be saved, and thy house.
—Acts 16:31

The only way to salvation is through believing.

For by grace are ye saved through faith;
and that not of yourselves: it is the gift of God:
Not of works, lest any man should boast.
—Ephesians 2:8–9

We must trust in Jesus alone for our salvation.

> Neither is there salvation in any other: for there is
> none other name under heaven given among men,
> whereby we must be saved.
> *–Acts 4:12*

I invite you to claim victory over death. Claim Jesus as your personal Lord and Savior. Can you hear that small voice saying, "Come unto me"?

Are you willing to humble yourself and say, "Yes, I am a sinner who is lost"?

Pause and ask God to cover your sin debt and let Him know that you believe that He is a living God who wants to have a relationship with you. The crucifixion was meant to bring an end, but it marked the beginning of God's plan.

Today can mark the beginning of a new life, new light, and eternal hope for you! It is simple. Ask and believe and you shall be saved! He's already prepared the way.

ABOUT THE AUTHOR

K urt Pangborn is a collegiate athletics professional at Indiana University in Bloomington, Indiana. Serving as Assistant Director for Athletic Tours and Ticket Operations, Kurt specializes in customer care, promotion, and revenue generation. With over a decade of experience in collegiate athletics, he has built a foundation for achievement inside the industry. Success within the competition, sales, and advancement have been direct contributors from the workplace. Yet, claiming victory in all aspects of his life originated from his physical limitation.

Kurt's interests have stayed within the athletics and sports realm. Traveling to NASCAR races and baseball parks are a staple of his summer travel plans. When at home, Kurt enjoys spending time on the lake fishing, serving at his home church, connecting with friends, and spending time in the kitchen cooking. Through professional speaking, he hopes to travel the world and use his voice to serve others, developing friendships for eternity.

From a beginning that put his sight into question, a vision was developed that turned out far greater than any physical sight. Kurt Pangborn, a man who entered life with the diagnosis of congenital glaucoma, has endured forty eye operations. Through talented physicians, dedicated peers, and an ever-faithful God, Kurt continues to overcome. Illuminated in Kurt's character is a desire to reach the thousands who are living with a disability, along with millions of individuals who are overcome with fear from the global pandemic and faced with an unknown tomorrow. Reaching all spectrums and ages through professional speaking, Kurt seeks to enact change through his powerful testimony.

Please visit www.kurtpangbornspeaks.com and learn how he can serve and present at your next event!

A free ebook edition is available with the purchase of this book.

To claim your free ebook edition:

1. Visit MorganJamesBOGO.com
2. Sign your name CLEARLY in the space
3. Complete the form and submit a photo of the entire copyright page
4. You or your friend can download the ebook to your preferred device

Morgan James BOGO™

A **FREE** ebook edition is available for you or a friend with the purchase of this print book.

CLEARLY SIGN YOUR NAME ABOVE

Instructions to claim your free ebook edition:
1. Visit MorganJamesBOGO.com
2. Sign your name CLEARLY in the space above
3. Complete the form and submit a photo of this entire page
4. You or your friend can download the ebook to your preferred device

Print & Digital Together Forever.

Snap a photo

Free ebook

Read anywhere

CPSIA information can be obtained
at www.ICGtesting.com
Printed in the USA
JSHW061417130722
28065JS00001B/12

9 781631 958175